BOB WILSON:

FROM PIT TO PULPIT

Written and Compiled by

Joy Wilson

A commissioned publication

23 Park Road, Ilkeston, Derbys DE7 5DA
Tel: 0115 932 0643 www.moorleys.co.uk

Dedicated
To each one of Bob's children:
Paul, John, David, Rachael and Sarah.

ISBN 978 086071 633 4

British Library Cataloguing in Publication Data.
A catalogue record for this book is available
from the British Library.

Printed from data supplied electronically

23 Park Road, Ilkeston, Derbys DE7 5DA
Tel: 0115 932 0643 www.moorleys.co.uk

Chapter One

It is amazing how one day can change your life; in fact things can change dramatically in just a few seconds. The 11th June 1968 was one such day, a day that was normal in every respect. It is true that there was a sense of expectation in the air, because that evening, we were expecting a visitor we had never met before.

My Mother and I lived in Harrow, which, at that time, was part of the London Northwest District of the Methodist Church of Great Britain. The annual Conference is the governing body of the Methodist Church, and all decisions are debated and ratified there; it is also the only time that ordinations take place. The venue changes from year to year, and in 1968, Conference met at The Central Hall, Westminster, London. When the appeal went out for people to offer accommodation for representatives to the Conference, my Mother felt that it was something we could do. In due course, we were told to expect the Reverend Robert Wilson.

And so, although we knew he wouldn't be arriving until the evening, the day was spent in making sure everything was in place. We knew nothing about him - not even his age. When he arrived, we discovered that he was in his thirties, and a Probationer Minister, which means that he had not yet been ordained. He had travelled directly from Rydal, in the Lake District, where he had been on 'Ordinands Retreat'.

We quickly discovered that he had a great sense of humour, when we learned that on the journey to London with three of his college friends, he had become separated from the others. When the train had reached Sheffield, they were all feeling a little hungry, and so Bob was dispatched to get some food and drink while the train was in the station. As he dashed back to the now moving train, he was unable to board it with arms full of bags of crisps and drinks, and he watched in dismay, as his friends and his luggage disappeared into the distance.

He always commented on how lonely he felt at that moment; but it all worked out in the end, because, after about an hour's wait, he caught an express train to London, which arrived less than 10 minutes behind the original one, and the four friends were reunited. On top of that, he had feasted on the food and drink as he waited!

And so, at about 8p.m. that evening, Bob arrived at our home, to be greeted by my mother and sister-in-law, Norma. While Mum was making a cup of tea, Norma chatted to Bob. Searching for something to say, she asked Bob what his work had been before going into the Ministry, when he said he had been a coal miner, she replied: "Well, you've got a cleaner job now!" This amused Bob greatly, and he never forgot it.

From our home in Harrow, Westminster was a fairly easy journey on the London Underground. Bob was attending because he was to be "Received into full Connexion" and Ordained. For him, it was the beginning of the work he loved passionately, and to which he gave himself wholeheartedly for the rest of his life. Ordination also marked the culmination of many years of academic struggle and sheer hard work. The strength of character, and single mindedness in following his dream, came from his upbringing, for both his parents had great determination; although his Mother was the powerhouse of the family. They had very little money, but it was well compensated for, by the resolve bred into all the children, to do your best with what you've got.

Robert Wilson was born on 22nd December 1934. He was the youngest of six children (3 boys and 3 girls) all born within 7 years and 1 month, to Ann and John Wilson. Both parents worked on the farm, so Bob was born in a tied cottage belonging to Pattisons Farm, in the hamlet of Red Row, just on the edge of the small town of Bedlington, Northumberland. Red Row consisted of one row of houses and two farms, and was about one and a half miles north east of the town centre.

His mother remembered that she had a difficult birth with Robert (as she always called him), and that he weighed 10lb. He was baptised at St John's Anglican Church at Bedlington Station - the nearest part of the town to Red Row; his brothers and sisters were all baptised there.

By the time he was 2½ years old, a small Mission Chapel had been opened at Red Row, and his parents attended there until it closed, many years later. All the children went to Sunday School, but Bob opted out when he was about 11 years old. He always said that it coincided with the advent of his first pair of long trousers, and at that point, he thought he was too grown up for Sunday School!

The local school, Barrington, was quite a walk from Red Row across 3 fields but Bob was taken there by his brothers and sisters, and brought home each day for lunch. On days when the weather was bad, his Mam would walk to the school with their lunches, to save them getting wet and cold. Money was extremely scarce, and his mother took what work she could, including milking at the farm, cleaning, mending, washing and ironing. One of the children's teachers was heard to comment, "The Wilson children often come to school with a patch or a mend, but never a hole!"

School holidays were spent on the beach at Cambois (pronounced Cammis), just over 2 miles away, as the crow flies. Every day for 5 weeks, weather permitting, their Mam packed up their lunch and tea, and walked them there and back, initially with 2 children in the pram, 2 on the pram in a makeshift seat, and 2 walking. On one, rare, occasion, they ventured further afield, and went to Newbiggin-by-the-Sea about 5 miles away, this time by train, but Edna, the eldest, shut her finger in the train door, and hurt it badly, so it was not a very happy day, and they did not return for a long time.

It was therefore amazing, if not miraculous, that his mother, by sheer determination and hard work, managed to save the deposit for a house by the time Bob was 10 years old, and so they left Red Row and moved to number 11, Rothesay Terrace, at Bedlington Station, about a mile closer to the town than Red Row.

In September 1946, Bob took his place at "Bedlington Station Modern School". His first school report comments that he "talks too much", but in all subjects except music, he did well, gaining first place in the class for geography. By the end of that school year, he was a member of the House Cricket and Football teams, and, with regard to his conduct, the report states "somewhat aggressive at times towards his fellow class mates". His final report was excellent, stating that he "takes a full part in school life" and that he was "a steady, reliable boy". Bob's school memories differed somewhat from that. He remembered being told, frequently, that his behaviour was not up to that of his brothers and sisters - which had irritated him intensely - and that he was always in fights - 'a bit of a tear-away'. His mother just said that he was not perfect, and a 'bit of a rascal'.

Bob was always a keen sportsman; he is second from the left in both pictures

6

Don and Mary [Bob's sister] with Gillian in the middle, and Joy on the right.

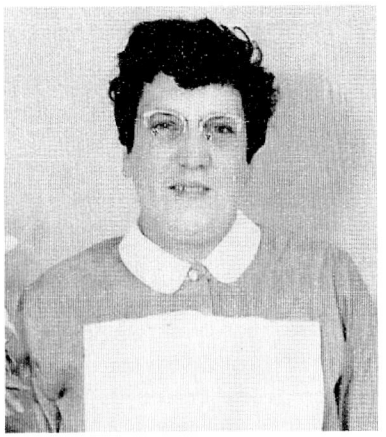

Mum and Dad   *Bob's sister, Edna*

Brother-in-law Jack with Joy, Rachael and Sarah, with sister Jean

Above: Bob with sister-in-law Norma, brother John and Joy

Brother William with his wife Sheila

8

Bob is in the back row, second from right, at this meeting of young, new Christians in his home Circuit.

Chapter Two

At 15, the school leaving age at that time, Bob couldn't wait to get out and start work. The main industry, in the whole of the area, was coal mining, but his grandfather, and many other relatives, had died in pit accidents, and his parents didn't want any of the boys to go 'down the pit'. The eldest boy, John, served his National Service in the navy, and spent most of his working life at Wilkinson Sword. William, served in the army, and trained as a carpenter. The girls, Edna, Jean and Mary, began their working lives in shops. Edna later became a very highly regarded nursing sister in the mental hospital at Morpeth.

All looked good for Bob. He began an apprenticeship with a small local family firm of electricians called Mood. The workforce consisted of a father and his two sons, and Bob. The pay was very low, about £1 per week, but at the end of a year, the business failed, and Bob was without a job.

Harry Tate was a close friend at that time; they had been through school together, and were inseparable. Almost every photograph taken of Bob at that time has Harry in it too! Harry had left school, and gone straight to the pit, as had several other friends. Coal miners in those days were relatively well paid, and Bob was envious of his friends who had plenty of money - or at least enough to do what they liked, when they liked. His 'excuse' for going to the pit was always that 'there was nothing else', but his mother remembered that the pay had a great deal to do with the decision.

Many people have assumed, down the years, that Bob was a Bevin Boy, but he was always adamant that he wasn't. Bevin Boys came into being in the 1940's, at the height of the Second World War, when there was a real crisis in providing the huge amount of power needed to keep British Industry going. Initially, a ballot was taken of all men eligible for conscription, and a certain number were sent to the coal mines; the rest joined the Army, Navy or Air Force. Later on, the ballot was dropped, and men could opt to go to the mines rather than the Armed Forces. Many Conscientious Objectors chose to work in the pits.

Bevin Boys were restricted in the sort of work they were allowed to do, and it was only full-time employees who were able to work on the coal face itself; wages were obviously higher for them than the Bevin Boys. Bob joined the pit because he wanted to, and was always a long-term member of the work force, although, when he was eligible, by age, for National Service, he was, in fact, exempt as a coal miner.

Work in the pit was extremely hard, and, because of all the dangers, there were strict rules. For example, no litter was allowed to be left lying around, because of the danger of fire, and, for the same reason, miners were searched at the beginning of a shift, to make sure that they had no cigarettes or matches on them. Also, originally for the same sort of reasons, I assume, there was a tremendous pit hierarchy, with the pit deputy (foreman) holding quite a powerful position. It was Bob's experience that only the deputy had the safety lamp with which gas could be detected, although all pits differ from each other in their routines.

All miners were given a tag as they went on shift; by this means the officials knew who was underground at any time, and this was of great importance at times of mine accidents. Bob was never in a major accident, but there were always minor mishaps, and Bob was involved in many of these. He was always proud of his blue scars - made by coal dust in a wound - and of one on his nose especially, because he got financial compensation for it (£25).

All miners who go underground work in shifts. The one most hated was the winter day shift, when they went to work in the dark and came home in the dark, and had been in the dark all day. Many miners, Bob included, would make use of sun lamps when they were off duty, and Bob never forgot the day he fell asleep under his - with sunglasses on - and looked like a panda for days! He even resorted to his sister's make-up to try to tone it down!! I'm sure that it was because of the years underground, that Bob loved the beauty of nature, and especially the sun. Later in life, he would work in the sun, at every opportunity. It was not unusual to see him in the back garden, stripped to the waist, and typing away at the next Sunday's sermon.

It often took a while to get to the coal face, and so the actual hard work on each shift was not the full 8 hours. Bob told of travelling a couple of miles (Sometimes by 'train' - coal tubs providing the carriages) to the start of a shift. The work was solid slog once they arrived, with only a brief lunch break. Obviously, everyone had a packed lunch - known as bait - and it was eaten where they were. Bob virtually always had bread and butter and sugar sandwiches, with a Thermos of hot, sweet tea or hot chocolate. Plenty of water was also essential, because of the danger of dehydration, with all the sweat shed in sheer, physical hard work, and also because it is quite warm underground. Men would eat their sandwiches to the last corner, having made sure that that was the only part of the bread that they had touched, and then it would be thrown away. This encouraged many mice and rats. Bob used to say that they were a great problem after a two-week shut down for holidays, because they were desperate for food. The pit ponies were sometimes a problem after a break, too - they didn't take kindly to going underground again after a spell in the fresh air. Bob always steered clear of them, and I'm sure many others did too.

Miners in Bob's day were very superstitious; there was always a great reluctance to work on the first day back, after a break, and in later years, Bob would often joke - "Don't wash my back - you'll weaken my spine!" This was a throwback to his mining years.

Bob had not worked at the pit for very long, when he requested to be put to work right on the coal face - because the pay was so much better (danger money!) and he ended up there for over seven years! The coal face was many, many yards wide, but often less than 2 feet 6 inches high. The coal cutting machine would go in first to loosen and cut the coal, then the miners, lying on their sides most of the time, and working with a pick, would start to move the coal out. At certain times work would stop, while hydraulic pit props were put in, to secure the roof.

The coal mine, like everywhere else, has its own sounds, and the workers get used to them, and learn to "read" them. Creaks and groans from the beams become friends, and unusual sounds act as early warning systems. Miners too learn very quickly that their own safety does not only depend on reading the signs and sounds underground, but also on their own work mates. There may be disagreements on the surface, but each man must trust his colleagues implicitly - his life may one day depend on it.

The mine brings everything down to one basic level. It is difficult to keep up appearances when you are covered from head to toe in coal dust, dressed in the oldest clothes you possess, and having to cope with the most basic human habits from the rest of your shift, as well as deal with your own, and if you do anything daft, you have to live with the teasing and leg-pulling for weeks on end!

Bob spoke of his experience in the pit, in an early sermon entitled "Black Diamond".

I want you to use your imagination for a moment, as I conduct you on a tour of a pit. In fact, the one in which I worked for 10 years. On arrival at the Pithead Baths, you change into your pit clothes, which include knee pads for kneeling on, and a safety helmet. From the baths you then go to the Lamp Room, where you are issued with 2 lamps: a cap lamp attached to a battery, which hangs round the waist, and a safety lamp, which the Coal Miners Act requires among groups of men. From the Lamp Room, you make your way to the Pit Shaft where, after being searched, you then get into the lift affair to take you underground. I said lift affair. We called them cages - nothing like the lifts you find in hotels and department stores, and not as smooth running, either. Into this almost bare cage, would ride as many as 20 men.

At the shaft bottom, men would go in different directions, using various roadways to get to their particular places of work. Again, the distances vary. We used to walk 2 miles, in many places almost bent double, before we got to our working. On arrival, we would strip off our outer clothing, collect our gear, and then crawl on to the coal face. The seam on which we worked was only 2 feet 3 inches (high) so you were either kneeling or lying on your side to work. The ventilation was quite good, but this didn't stop you from sweating continuously, and then, ending the shift, being black from head to toe. A mad dash to the pit shaft bottom, and then the cage back to the surface: the welcome shower bath, and then home to a big dinner.

By and large, most miners are hardworking and conscientious when they are at work. Most people think of miners as big, strapping men. Of course some are, but there are a lot of miners who are thin and wiry. Slimming is no problem when you sweat for 7 hours on the trot. The miner himself is usually pale-faced through lack of sunshine. It's a fact, that in the winter, depending on your shift, that you see little daylight. It may be light when you go to work in the morning, but when you come to the surface at the end of the shift, it's dark again. In the summer, it's an awful feeling to sit at the Pithead in warm sunshine, and then, within a few minutes, you go into another world, where, summer and winter alike, conditions remain the same.

Chapter Three

For 10 years, from the age of 16, Bob worked in the pit. He had money to "jingle in his pocket", which was his chief aim, and he was out to enjoy life, and enjoy life he did - to the full! He was the first to admit that he worked hard and played hard.

Much of a miner's social behaviour is an escape from the risks and uncertainties that mining brings. Quoting from "Black Diamond" Bob says:-

> In my own family, there have been fatal accidents on both sides. My Grandfather and Uncle were both killed in the pit, whilst my wife's Uncle was also killed in a mine accident. Very few miners who work for a life time, escape without some mark or scar to remind them of an accident. From the moment you step into the lift to take you underground, you become involved in the risks and dangers of mining.

> The charge has often been levelled at the miner that he's never content, that he spends every ha'penny he gets on drinking and gambling - that every moment away from the Pit is an attempt to find satisfaction and fulfilment. I'm not excusing the miner for this way of living, but I sincerely believe that this search for thrills and new experiences outside of work, stems from the risks and uncertainties which mining brings. Perhaps the miner would never openly admit this, but his attempts to escape his environment are such, that all kinds of things are tried. Underlying his actions (always subconsciously) but never expressed verbally, is the feeling that perhaps this next shift might be the last.

Bob was no exception. He drank, often to excess; he smoked, and generally painted the town red. He did give up drinking, though, after a night out when he drank so much that he vomited all over the brand new suit, that he was wearing for the first time! He had it dry-cleaned, but the stain never came out, and it put him off alcohol for the rest of his life. Smoking, too, was given up before it became a lifelong habit.

Working in the pit was a memory that never left Bob; later in life, he always looked for a piece of coal on the Communion Table as part of the Harvest display; in fact, on one occasion, he complained [in a jokey way] that there was no coal, and in the evening, nearly fell over a box of coal that had been placed on the pulpit steps!

In his late teens, he met the girl who was to become his first wife; she came from the neighbouring mining town of Ashington, and they spent most nights dancing. Bob was happy enough to do this at the time, but it put him off ballroom dancing for the rest of his life! From that point on, his friends from the pit began to fade from his social life, and all his spare time was spent with his girlfriend. They married in 1956, and began married life with Bob's parents.

The house in Rothesay Terrace was actually 2 self-contained flats. When the family first moved in (1944), the top flat was let, and the 8 members of the Wilson family lived downstairs. The 3 boys had one room, the 3 girls had another, and Mum and Dad, another. Everything else took place in either the living room or the kitchen - there was no bathroom. Each of the bedrooms really only had enough room for a double bed, and the living room was not much bigger. It is amazing how they ever coped. As the family gradually moved out, Mum and Dad were able to spread themselves, bit by bit. By the time Bob was married, Mary, the next youngest to Bob, was married to Don, also a pit worker, and they were living in the upstairs flat.

Bob and Don got on exceptionally well, as did their two wives, and they became quite a foursome, even spending holidays together when they both had young families. By the late summer of 1956, Mary and Don had a baby girl, Gillian, and a first child was on the way for Bob and his wife. Everything in the garden was rosy, but Don was dealt a series of devastating blows.

He had been brought up by a stepmother, believing that his real mother had died when he was very young, but that summer, someone said something to him, that at first set him thinking, and then, into action. He found out that his mother had not died all those years ago, but that she was alive and well in a mental hospital only a few miles away. She had been taken ill with post natal depression after the birth of Don's younger brother, and admitted to hospital; somehow, her presence there had been overlooked, and no-one signed the forms for her release when she became fit. Once Don had found her, he and his brothers were able to obtain her release, almost immediately.

As if this was not a big enough shock, almost immediately after his mother's release, Don's father had a massive heart attack and died. Neither Don nor Bob realised it at the time, but this was to be the beginning of the greatest turning point, not only of their lives, but in the lives of many other people too.

Don was very badly affected, and, in his despair, tried to find some answers to all that had happened. To try to make sense of these events, he turned to the Bible. He had never been to Sunday School, and had had a totally non-Christian upbringing, with no Church links at all, but he read the Bible through, from Genesis to Revelation, with only the Holy Spirit to guide him. He was not yet aware of it, but the Holy Spirit was already working away in his life, and most importantly, his mind; at the same time, the Holy Spirit was working in Bob's subconscious too.

Having read the small, pocket King James Bible that he had bought himself, Don reached the conclusion, that if what Jesus said about himself, and what Paul and others said about Jesus was true, then in 1956, Jesus could change lives as he did when he walked the highways and byways of Palestine almost 2,000 years ago.

One Sunday morning, Don was sitting on a park bench very close to a Methodist Church in Bedlington town centre. The town was fairly quiet, and, as he sat there, he heard the sound of singing drifting from the church, across the town streets. The singing sounded so attractive, that he got up, wandered in, and sat at the back for the rest of the service, but worship seemed very strange to him, and so, during the week, he asked Bob if he would go with him on the next Sunday morning. Let me tell you the rest in Bob's own words.

> *Instead of a discourteous 'No', I said 'Yes', and for several weeks, this was our lifestyle. We attended church regularly. I began to get a little worried when, after a service, as we walked home together, Don would be discussing the sermon, and how God was speaking to him. I began to get cold feet! I'd heard of people who were religious fanatics, and I didn't want to be one of them, but out of a deep respect for my brother-in-law, I continued to attend.*

And then, on the evening of 16th December 1956, after the Church Service, the Youth Fellowship of the Circuit were watching a film depicting the life of John Wesley, and, at the end, the young probationer Minister - Rev Bernard Moss - made an evangelistic appeal: 'Would those who felt they wanted to commit their lives to Jesus, come forward.' In all, 18 people responded, amongst them, 2 young coal miners who had found grace in Jesus.

Imagine, then, the situation, after a Sunday evening like that, to get up and go to work on the Monday morning, let alone face your own team of tough, down-to-earth coal miners! I don't know how Don coped with all that, but Bob said:

After that, things could never be the same again. I had had a Christian experience - the next day, I would be at my place of work, 1,000 feet underground, on a coal face less than 2 feet 6 inches high and there to live out my faith. It wasn't easy, but God was faithful.
'Bob,' my work mates said, when I told them that Jesus was my Saviour, 'We'll give you a month, we'll give you 3 months, you'll never live out your experience here'. Well, it was hard and tough, but those work mates of mine had to admit that there was a change in my life that defied human explanation.

That following September (1957) saw Don as a student at Cliff College, from there, he and his family went to Shetland for two years as a Lay Pastor, and then on to theological training at Wesley College, Headingly, Leeds. Immediately his training at college was finished, he was sent to India, and served the Methodist Church there, but life was hard, especially for Mary. They firstly had to learn Hindi, as Bob remembered at the Thanksgiving Service for Mary's life in 1985, at which he both led and preached:

How we laughed and commented at the time 'What a pity they didn't speak Geordie out in India!' Mary would have been well away, for it was true, that, wherever she was in the world, in Shetland, or Leeds, or India, or Wallsend, or Hawes, or the United States, or Seahouses, Mary never lost her Geordie, or more correctly, her Northumbrian accent.

But it was in India that Mary gave birth to twin boys, Peter and Andrew, who joined their two little girls, Gillian and Joy. At the age of 4 months, Andrew was bitten by a mosquito and died 14th December 1964. Bob commented: *"Mary was to leave part of herself in a strange land."*

On their return from India, Don, was stationed at Wallsend-on-Tyne - stationing being the Methodist term for placing Ministers in appointments. Wallsend was not the happiest time of their Ministry and before too long, they moved again, this time to Hawes, a picturesque market town in Wensleydale, North Yorkshire. They fell in love with the people, the lifestyle and the countryside, and were there for quite a long stay in Methodist terms. After a year's Exchange of Pastorates to North Rose, Northern New York State, U.S.A., Don transferred to the United Methodist Church, and after one year back in Hawes, went out for good in the summer of 1976, this time to Potsdam, not too far from North Rose. Unfortunately this time was all too short. Don became unwell in September 1978, and they decided to return home to the two girls, who were now established with their own homes in Epsom, Surrey.

In September 1979, Don and Mary were stationed at Seahouses in Northumberland, and Don was recognised as a Minister on loan from the United Methodist Church. When it became difficult for him to transfer back into British Methodism, Don resigned, and they moved out of the Manse and into a home nearby. In November 1984, Don was taken into St Thomas' Hospital in London for heart surgery. There were various complications, and he was still there in January, when Mary was diagnosed with stomach cancer, and given just one month to live. Don was allowed out of hospital to sit with her. In one of Mary's last letters, written to a friend, she said *"I have an ulcer, and cancer of the stomach, and I only have weeks to live, but I also have Jesus'.* This made a profound impression on Bob; he said at her Thanksgiving Service:

> *When we knew of Mary's condition, we visited her every week in the hospital in Epsom, and, on those brief visits, I felt we were even closer to her. Between our last visit and last but one, I wrote a letter to Mary, saying that Joy and I hoped to bring Rachael and Sarah with us, as it was the half-term break, and would she like me to bring the Bread and the Wine for Holy Communion. If she felt up to it on the day, we would all celebrate together.*

> *When we arrived on the Thursday, the day before she died, we knew she was much weaker, and Joy and the girls were quite*

prepared to wait in the car park. When I went in with Don, Mary's first question was: 'Where's Joy and the girls? I'd like to see them'. She also asked, 'Rob, have you brought the Communion?'

It was a marvellous moment, and an unforgettable experience. Mary was in bed in a very weak condition; around the bed were gathered 5 of us, Don, Joy, our two daughters, Rachael and Sarah, and me. We shared those symbols of Bread and Wine, and we reminded ourselves of Christ's Passion, Death and Resurrection. When the Communion was over, we kissed Mary for the last time, before making our way back the 110 miles to Cheltenham.

Mary died, late in the evening, the following day, 22nd February 1985.

Don was lost without her, and the following year, April 1986, he went back to North Rose for a holiday. There, he renewed his friendship with many people, including Ginny, whom he married in September that year. He carried on his ministry in U.S.A. as far as his health would allow it, concentrating a lot on Christian Counselling. On 17th January 1995, Don had a massive heart attack, and died at his home in North Rose.

I have felt it important to give a brief account of Don and Mary's ministry, because so much of Bob was caught up with them, especially in the early days, and Bob never ever forgot the debt he owed Don for bringing him to know Jesus.

Bob and Don's Conversion experience spilled over to the rest of the family, making a tremendous impact on Mary, as we have seen, and also, later, on Edna. But for Bob it was back to the daily grind of life underground. He said, in the sermon, "Black Diamond":

For the Christian working in a pit, will bring him into a man's world, where life is hard and tough - where the language is as strong as you'll find anywhere - perhaps stronger. And yet, despite this, there can be a wonderful sense of comradeship - particularly so, when conditions are really bad, or when someone is injured. The very best is brought out of men, who, outwardly appear to be cursing, swearing miners. Such men can see the sham in much religion professed by some, but whose lives are far from the truth or the mind of Jesus. The thing I learned most of all was this: that what these men wanted was to see Christianity in action, and not just Sunday religion, but to see Christianity in action when you find yourself crawling around on a coal face. I thank God that I experienced life as a miner from both sides, before I became a Christian, and afterwards. It's not enough to say 'Oh yes! I'm a Christian!' It has to be seen in the way we live, and do our work - in our attitudes to life itself.

How did this affect my own experience? As a Christian, I soon discovered that, in Christ, life takes on a new meaning, and even work which was hard and gruelling could become purposeful. My experience before my conversion was to fill my life with anything and everything, in an attempt to escape - in an attempt to find fulfilment. But life in Christ, or eternal life, is of such quality that it is carried into the very hardest of tasks. I'm not going to say I enjoyed working in the Pit, for that would be the wrong use of the word 'enjoy', but I can honestly say that I had satisfaction, and could see some purpose, and only hoped and prayed that others might find new life in Christ.

For a while, Bob was quite happy, working in the Pit and serving in the local Methodist Church, but one day, he felt that God was calling him to preach. His name went forward, and he was given 'a Note to Preach' - literally a letter from the Superintendent Minister of his Circuit, giving him permission to go out with a 'Fully Accredited Local Preacher' and share in the responsibilities of leading worship. Bob was appointed to Charlie Dott, whom he both liked and admired, and looked back at that time with great affection. Once he was considered competent enough to lead worship on his own, he became an 'On Trial', which meant that his services were reported on regularly, and he was closely watched; mainly by other Local Preachers.

All preachers remain On Trial until they have completed and passed all the examinations set by the Methodist Church. In Bob's day there were three written examinations and an Oral Examination. For a miner, the day's work is very hard and demanding, as we have already seen, but it is all the more difficult when a regime of study is added, and Bob did find it tough going. He said *"The studies seemed impossible, and the only way I could do it, was to go to bed early in the evening, get up early in the morning, and do two hours study each day. I passed all my exams - only 3 in those days, and in June 1959, I became a Fully Accredited Methodist Local Preacher."*

On Mission from Cliff College at Morecambe 1961

From the left: Joy, Bob, Ivan Wilson, and wife Zandra

Bob at Headingley

*The Tea Club.
From the left: Neville Whitehead, Bob,
John Barrell, Martin Eggleton*

*Headingley Theological College, Leeds. Bob is in the centre, third row back.
Don Robinson is in the front row, far left.*

At Headingley – Bob is second from the left, back row

Headingley - Bob is in the third row from the front, in the middle.

*The centenary dinner at Carclaze Methodist Church,
in the St Austell Circuit 1970*

Bob, at work as an Industrial Chaplain, at Scammells, Watford.

Chapter Four

But the call, by then, to go on further, was beginning to tug at him, and so, like Don before him, he applied to go to Cliff College in Derbyshire. He was accepted and in September 1960, he left the Pit for the last time, and became a student all over again.

Cliff College is situated in the Peak District of Derbyshire, and is a Christian training college for men and women, although, in Bob's day, it was men only. Cliff is a Methodist college, but members of other Churches are welcome. Students used to stay for one year, with a few staying for a second to take a course in Evangelism. Over the years, Cliff has changed and grown in the range of courses offered, and nowadays it is linked to Manchester University. So in addition to open access foundation courses students can obtain degrees at all levels. Bob never ever stopped singing its praises, and he always said that, in his day, they took tough, poorly educated young men, and trained them into Christians who would be of great use to the Church.

Many students go there, even today, to examine their lives and to sort out where they stand in their faith, to seek to listen to the Lord, and to understand what work He is calling them to do. Many will go back to their local Churches with renewed vigour; others will find work with a Christian bias, for example, Langley House Trust, who work with ex-prisoners; or perhaps the Probation Service. For some it will be a calling to full-time Christian work as Lay Workers, evangelists or youth workers, but for a good proportion, the future will eventually lead them into the Full Time Ministry, as it did with both Bob and Don. The Principal in Bob's day was Rev Tom Meadley, whom he admired more than words can say, and he never forgot the debt he owed him, and Tom never forgot him, either. It was to be 20 years, after Bob left Cliff, before they met again, and Tom recognised him immediately - and knew his name - Bob was thrilled!

Many students have said, even in recent years, that their time at Cliff was the hardest of their life, but the one that they wouldn't have missed for the world. Bob felt exactly the same. He found the studying hard, and the manual work, that every student is expected to do, not particularly his 'cup of tea', but it was a good grounding for the future. The actual work on Mission Teams was hard and challenging, but that, too, prepared him for the future. But the most valuable experience of all, was the time to think, to spend time with his Lord, and to slowly make the decision to offer for the full time ministry.

Bob, like students before and since, found that the "Cliff Experience" is special, and even those who were not close during their time there, share a real bond and camaraderie. Bob kept a very casual contact with quite a few students, but one in particular remained a friend for the rest of his life. Ivan Wilson (no relation) came from St Vincent in the West Indies to study at Cliff, and then went on to train for the Methodist Ministry in this country. After many years, he went to work in Saskatoon, Saskatchewan, Canada. He writes:-

I'm not the best one for anecdotes. I just remember him as a wonderful friend to me, and all the men at Cliff, when we were there. Immediately we arrived at Cliff in September 1960, he took me under his wing, and would look out for my needs and my interests. A peasant, and a miner, we were the humblest folk there, and so there was a special bond between us. He would always include me in whatever he was doing, and wherever he was going. We had a great time at Morecambe on trek. He was the cook for the group. The Sheffield hurricane did a great deal of damage. At Cliff many trees fell, and Robbie, who used to work outdoors at one of the tutors' gardens made a cross from two twigs to hang in his room. He also brought me two pieces too, for me to make a cross. He drove a nail in the two pieces of twigs, and made a simple, rugged cross for me. I have carried it all these years, or rather, it has carried me, and now it hangs over my desk, in my office. It is a pity our paths never crossed after we left Cliff. We went to different Colleges, he to Headingly in Leeds, and I, to Hartley Victoria in Manchester, and we served in different Districts, but the friendship formed when we were both freshmen at Cliff has not diminished by time or distance .

Did you know he took me to his home in (near) Morpeth my first Christmas at Cliff? Christmas? He took me down the coal mine where he used to work right to the coal face, and showed me how the men had to work, lying on their back, and load their coal, to be carried back to the surface by the ponies. After that experience, I thought, in later years, the miners deserved every penny Joe Gormley and Arthur Scargill were able to negotiate for them. The work those men had to do was like the slavery that black people endured, excepting for the lashings the blacks got as well, for their pains. Robbie never forgot his life in the mine, and it was the inspiration for his gratitude and faithfulness in Ministry. His time at Cliff and in College, took a great toll on his family. It is never easy to live in reduced circumstances, it is hard enough when they are unavoidable, but when one chooses them for one's self, and thereby involve others, it is doubly hard, because one has to live with the situation and the guilt of not being able to provide as well as one would like for one's family.

Ivan's deep felt comments, as he compared coal mining with slavery, have even more power, when you know that Ivan himself, is a black West Indian.

The time "On Trek" was a wonderful memory for Bob, too. Even today, all Cliff students go on a 3 week mission each summer, nowadays they tend to have a somewhat more comfortable life style, and Bob would delight in telling any he came across, that they had it 'cushy' now. In 1960, they were issued with a uniform, khaki shorts and shirts - and a "trek cart" - rather like a huge wooden two-wheeled, wheelbarrow, which was pulled along by several men, these were dismantled and put on a coach, and men and cart, unloaded at their destination. "Home" for those 3 weeks at Morecambe, was a Church Hall. - As Ivan said, Bob was cook for the group, but he found it frustrating, as he could only cook the food provided for the team by sympathetic locals. Ivan seemed to attract a lot of bananas! He took a lot of convincing that they were meant for the whole group - not just for himself! Bob remembered –'a few heated disagreements' about that. But without a doubt, it did the team the world of good, and stood them all in good stead for wherever the Lord was to lead them, and with the passage of time, the memories became mellow and precious.

The cross that Bob made for himself, still hangs in our study, and any Cliff students that visit, recognise it immediately, so it must be a sort of ritual that they all make one!

Bob used his time of study at Cliff to prepare himself, academically, for the following year, when he would offer for the full-time ministry. He had to re-sit his Old Testament Local Preachers examination, and also start to 'knuckle down' to revision etc. for the examinations that were to come. Without a doubt, this year was invaluable, in the transition from miner to full-time student.

Bob left Cliff at the beginning of August 1961, and went back to his home and family in Bedlington. He found a job via a friend, in a local mental hospital, St George's at Morpeth, about 5 miles from Bedlington. There, they knew that his aim was to train as a Methodist Minister, and gave him all the help they could; he was allowed to observe most of the treatments, and to spend as much time as he liked, talking to patients. He often referred to his time there.

In the Methodist Church, it takes almost a year to go through all the procedures needed to apply to train for the Ministry. It begins with the recommendations of the Church Council to send you forward to the Circuit Meeting, who, in turn, vote on whether to send you forward to the District Synod. At the same time, two candidates examinations have to be taken, one in Biblical Studies, and the other a General Knowledge paper, and also, two trial services. At the District Synod, the candidate is asked to give his/her testimony, and, after hearing that, seeing the examination results, and the marks for the trial services, the decision is made as to whether they go forward to the Connexional Candidates Committee. In Bob's time, this was called the 'July' Committee, but it met in June! Nowadays, it meets in April! If all goes well, and the candidate is accepted, he/she begins training the following autumn. This whole procedure is known as 'Candidating for the Ministry'. All in all, it is a very tough year, and for those who succeed, there is great elation, but those who are turned down, often find it hard to come to terms with the rejection, and to pick up the pieces and start their lives all over again.*
[The system is now very different, but still involves the Connexional Candidates Committee in April].

In 1961, when Bob candidated, there were only men accepted for training although we have now had women ministers for over 30 years. Bob was accepted at his first attempt, and he was sent to Headingley Theological College, Leeds. His studies began there in the autumn of 1962. Because he was married, Bob was allowed to live outside College, with his family, by now there were two little boys, Paul who was 4½ and John who was 2¼.

They found a flat not far from the College, and life settled down. Bob was allowed no concessions because he lived out, he had to be at the College in time for Morning Prayers, study in his room at College, and only go home at the end of the day. That home became a haven for many of the students. His wife found it very hard and lonely; but both she and Bob rejoiced when David was born in June, 1963, back in Bedlington.

Chapter Five

Bob found the studying extremely hard, and learning Greek totally impossible, after struggling with it for quite a period of time, he eventually plucked up courage to go and see the Principal, the Rev A Raymond George, M.A., B.D., and explained his difficulty. After a great deal of discussion, he was allowed to give up Greek, and replace it with further Biblical Studies. He often commented when telling this story, that after he had prepared the way, a whole stream of other men found their way to Raymond George's study to ask if they could exchange their Greek lessons for something else!

With the responsibility for a young, fast growing family, Bob worked as much as he possibly could in the College vacations. He worked on building sites, and did any work he was offered. Later on, he met June and Dennis Carter at their Church, when he was sent there to preach. He remembered, fondly, Christmas Eves spent with the family and of singing "Christians awake, salute the happy morn" at the stroke of midnight. From that moment on "Christians Awake" was always his first hymn at the Christmas Morning Service wherever he was.

The Carter family had a removal business, and Bob worked for them frequently. He learned techniques for carrying furniture that he never forgot, and never allowed me to forget either! Whenever we were carrying a heavy wardrobe or chest or bookcase, he would look for a piece of doweling, or a broom handle, he even used my rolling pin once! He would put it under the furniture and roll it across the floor. Always he would say: "Do it my way, I know what I'm doing. I used to work for a furniture remover, you know."

Sport always played a large part in Bob's life. As a young man in Bedlington, he had been, and was until his death, an ardent supporter of Newcastle United football team. With his move to Leeds, there came an affection for Leeds United, and Manchester United was followed avidly because of Bobby Charlton. Both Bobby and Jack, who at that time played for Leeds, were of a similar age to Bob, and came from the next pit village to Bob, Ashington. Bob had also done a little amateur boxing, but only had one official bout, which he lost; his comment later was "He didn't lay a punch on me - he couldn't catch me - I ran for 3 rounds!" To be fair, I think it was a mismatch; his opponent was vastly more experienced than Bob.

At Headingley, Bob was an eager and obvious choice for the Soccer 11, and, much to his delight, he was chosen as captain, a job that he took very seriously. In a report in the college magazine, 'ARK', for the 1963-1964 season, Bob wrote,

> The results of the 1963-64 season matched the very bad weather of the previous year, when during the Spring Term, no matches at all were played.

> The Autumn Term of '63 was a disastrous one indeed, for we were relegated to Division Two of the University Inter-Mural Soccer League. We played nine league matches and lost every one. The Spring Term of 1964 showed a slight improvement, for out of five league matches played, two were won, two were drawn, and one was lost.

> As was expected, both Hartley and Handsworth got their revenge by the odd goal, but the men of the Ark went down fighting.

> We look forward eagerly to the 1964-1965 season, and especially the inter-College games with Hartley and Handsworth, both of which will be played in the Spring Term. The fighting men of Wesley, who include five first year players, hope to restore the former glory.

Snooker was a hobby that Bob enjoyed throughout his ministry. At one time, it used to be said that if you were good at snooker it was a sign of a misspent youth, well, Bob spent a lot of time in the Y.M.C.A. in Bedlington, as all the teenaged lads did, and no doubt that was where his basic grounding in the game came from, but at Headingley he excelled himself, and won the Snooker Cup; a fact that he took great pride in re-telling.

Theological students are sent out to preach in local churches, and Bob had many tales to tell of his experiences. On one occasion, he preached in a well-heeled church in the only suit he possessed, a light grey one. The Church Stewards said nothing to him, but complained to Raymond George that he was not suitably dressed. Bob was very upset by this, especially as it was the best he had, and in the end, the whole student body was up in arms about it, threatening to boycott that particular church!

At Headingley, students were divided into small groups for study and relaxation. Bob's group of four consisted of John Barrell, E. Martin Eggleton, J. Neville Whitehead and Bob himself. This particular 'Tea Club' became firm friends, and although at times in later years the contact was very slim, they all took a great deal of interest in what was happening to each other. John Barrell sadly died a few years ago, but Bob was about to make contact with his widow, Pat, before he himself died. The Tea Club obviously all shared a great sense of humour, and Bob never forgot the Christmas Concert at Headingley one year, when they decided to mimic the Beatles, who were at the height of their career then. Everyone dressed up, and Bob, John and Neville had dyed floor mops to make the appropriate hairstyle, but not Martin, he combed all his hair forward, and cut it into a Beatle style!

Although academically, Bob obviously found Headingley hard, he enjoyed his time there, and revelled in the social activities, and the sport, and also appreciated the discipline. He never forgot Raymond George's words that at 9 a.m. you are to be in your study, with your shoes on (not slippers) and ready to work, thereby being ready to welcome anyone who calls; Bob always <u>was</u> ready at 9 a.m!

At times Bob felt inferior because of his lowly background and lack of academic qualifications, but he never dwelt on it, in fact he was always amazed at the way Cliff College had changed him from a rough coal miner into a person who was ready to train for the Methodist Ministry, and he was determined to make the most of that opportunity. By the time his training at Headingley was complete, he was ready, keen and eager to get on with his work.

Bob left Headingley in the summer of 1965, and he describes the final Service at the end of each College year as a very moving experience.

At Mary's Memorial Service, he said this:

> *I feel I ought to say something about Headingley days, and particularly the very end of our training at Wesley College..... permit me to mention another hymn, a great Charles Wesley hymn, in fact, our "old" College Hymn. Let me read slowly and carefully, those tremendous words:*

'Captain of Israel's Host, and Guide
Of all who seek the land above,
Beneath Thy shadow we abide,
The cloud of Thy protecting love;
Our strength, Thy grace; our rule, Thy word;
Our end, the glory of the Lord.

By Thine unerring Spirit led,
We shall not in the desert stray;
We shall not full direction need,
Nor miss our providential way:
As far from danger, as from fear,
While love, almighty love, is near'

I don't know how many times we sang that hymn during 3 years at Headingley – it must have been hundreds of times. But the most moving moment of any College year, was the very end, and the send-off given to those men who had completed their formal training, and who would soon be on their way to serve the Churches and Circuits of Methodism.

As the whole college gathered, the College Hymn, Captain of Israel's Host, would be sung over and over and over again, unaccompanied, until everyone of those leaving went with the Blessing of God, as well as the Blessing of 60 or 70 other Theological Students, together with the Principal and Tutors.

Captain of Israel's Host, from that point on, became Bob's favourite and it was taken to and used frequently in all the Circuits in which he served.

Shortly before the end of his training, Bob like all student ministers was asked what sort of appointment he felt he was called to. The questions asked were "This country or abroad; town or country?" Bob's reply - "This country, and a town" led him to Halifax. Initially he served and lived in the Hipperholme area, but a move within the Circuit (Halifax Wesley), meant that he served at West End and Fairfield Churches.

Chapter Six

Bob was told, before he started, that it was a difficult appointment, several of the Ministers who had immediately preceded him, had either left the ministry or had to pull out of the Circuit because of ill health, but Bob threw himself into the work with great gusto.

Peggy and Fred Titchmarsh, were very supportive during Bob's time in Halifax, sadly, they have both now gone to glory, but before her death, Peggy wrote about Bob: "Bob was always to be found at the Youth Club every Thursday night - Fred and I were helpers, but he was the mainstay, and he took great interest in the Boys Brigade at Fairfield. They were very fond of him, and appreciated his help and interest. He also started the giving of flowers on Mother's Day. He bought the daffodils, and a few of us put silver foil around 3 flowers and these were given to the mothers who were in church, by the children.

Members of the Mackintosh (sweet makers) family were also church members and Bob had very fond memories of going to tea with them. They sent one of their limousines to pick the family up, and Bob felt like royalty as they were driven through the town. When they were eating their tea, waited on by a maid, David, who was only 3 or 4 years old at the time, stole the show by asking, "When is the maid going to have her tea?" Bob never forgot the experience, and used the illustration widely, throughout his ministry.

But more than anything, Bob's abiding memory of Halifax, was the Long March. This was a sponsored walk to raise money for Christian Aid, which took place, through the night of Easter Day/Bank Holiday Monday, around the outskirts of the town (a full circle), and which covered 30 miles. It started at Easter 1965 and is still going strong. Bob even wrote a sermon about it, entitled "The Long March":

> ..... I want to liken the Christian life to the Long March of 1967, and consider some of the various aspects of the journey.
> ..... When we set off from the Odeon Cinema, a tremendous sense of enthusiasm and thrill was abroad. I'm quite sure that many of those young people had no idea of what lay ahead. Of course, there were the thrills, but there was also the other side of it. There were the uphill climbs which seemed to go on and on. At one

stage, we were not only climbing a steep hill, but were almost groping our way to the top: it was so badly lit. The stage of the journey which I consider the most difficult was the stretch of road from Salterhebble Hill along Elland Wood Bottom to Brighouse. The sheer monotony was almost too much, on a seemingly never-ending road. And yet it was important all along the 30 miles, not to look at the obstacles or the difficult stretches ahead, but to meet each one as it came.

There is also another side to the "Long March". There were the downhill stretches – times when you could almost "freewheel". There were the little 5 minute rests we took, every hour and a half, where we rested our weary legs. There were the added compensations of the Rest Centres, where cheerful ladies served refreshments, and we were able to sit comfortably, and regain some fresh energy and enthusiasm for the next stage of the journey.

The Christian life is a similar kind of journey. The Christian life is lived in this world, amidst the trials and difficulties of man's life. It isn't a bed of roses, and the sooner we wake up to this fact, the more ready we'll be in facing all that comes our way. There are the uphill climbs - times when everything seems against us. There are the dark places where we almost stumble and grope our way along. There are the times when we seem to be in a rut and feel like quitting - "We've had enough" ...But there are also the many joys and blessings of the Christian life. A deep sense of purpose, and a firm conviction that this life does matter - that this is the place where character is formed, and saints are made. The Christian life offers to man the Bread of Life; the sustenance necessary to complete the course. There are the Rest Centres, times when we need to stop and receive fresh supplies of energy and determination for the next stage of the journey.

There were people who said to me, when they heard that I had entered for the "Long March", "You'll never make it - you'll find it too exacting." On the journey there were people who were not officials, but simply onlookers, who jeered at us, as much as to say, you must be crazy for attempting to walk so far. But there were also people whose comments were really helpful and encouraging. As we walked up to the traffic lights at Queensbury, with still about 6 or 7 miles to go, we passed three people standing at the lights. One of them commented "You look good for another thirty miles". It was surprising how much that comment helped to boost our morale. During the 'March' you would probably find walkers in groups of two, three or four. In our own case, three of us were together for the last fifteen miles - there was a real sense of togetherness. We encouraged one another; we spurred one another on to greater effort, and it was amazing how important it was.

When I started out on the Christian life, I was 22 years old. There were those who laughed when I told them that I had become a Christian. There were others who said "You'll not last long - you'll never stick it out. You'll never live your Christian life here in the Pit". Those men were proved wrong. They said "We'll give you a month, three months, six months - it won't last." That was over ten years ago. It's important in the Christian life that we encourage one another, and have a sense of oneness - togetherness, so that we can overcome the difficulties and trials that come our way. Men laughed and jeered at Jesus, and finally crucified Him, but it did not deter Him from living out His life, and fulfilling His purpose. Jesus chose 12 disciples that they might be with Him - that they might share, intimately, their experience of life - that they might help and encourage one another, as they journeyed together.

From Queensbury traffic lights, we had another mile or so to go, up Denholme Gate Road, before we reached Raggalds Inn. A sharp left hand turn at the Raggalds, and we were on the home stretch, and walking towards Halifax. When we got through Ambler Thorn, we turned left again, and shortly after, we found ourselves walking down hill, with Halifax Town Centre clearly visible. We could see the flats in the Bus Station, the Town Hall; and, in our thoughts, the Y.M.C.A. and the FINISH.

A number of things were in my mind during those last two or three miles. Firstly, a tremendous sense of achievement, at having walked thirty miles in just under 8 hours, which included an hour and five minutes for stoppages – rests etc. We had averaged 4½ miles per hour over the thirty mile course.

Then there was the thought, that our efforts would not go unrewarded, but that we were raising money to help the *unfortunate war victims - orphans, widows in Vietnam. A real chance to think of others besides ourselves.*

Then there was the hot bath which was long overdue, and the prospect of lying for as long as possible in hot water. And finally, the rest from the ordeal of the 30 mile walk.

At the end of this sermon, are some figures, written in pencil, which appear to be the sums of money raised. Whether this was by Bob alone, by the members of the church, or by everyone on the March, I have no means of knowing, but the total of £15,100.00 was quite a sum in those days.

From 1965 until 1968, Bob's first 3 years in Circuit, he was also expected to do his 'probationer studies'. A Minister is not considered to be 'fully Qualified' until after Ordination, and up to that point the post college studies continue. This is a difficult time, because his/her 'normal' ministerial duties run side by side with the studies, and sometimes it's hard to fit everything in.

Chapter Seven

Perhaps at this point it would be useful to explain the "Circuit System" which is peculiar to the Methodist Church, and mainly the British Methodist Church.

Each geographical area throughout the country is divided into a Circuit. The Circuit will consist of a varying number of churches from as many as 37, which was the case in St Austell in 1970, to 12, which was the case in Cheltenham in 1979, and sometimes even less. Each Circuit has a number of ministers appointed - or stationed as Methodist terminology has it - and each minister has pastoral charge of one or more churches. One minister has overall responsibility, usually the one who is most experienced - or most 'years travelled' - and he is known as the Superintendent Minister.

Each Circuit belongs to a District, with pastoral oversight given to the District Chairman, [now there are women, it is referred to as 'Chair'] who is an ordained minister with several years experience. The Chairpersons meet together regularly, and are on Connexional Committees - Connexional being the term used for the whole of the Methodist Church under the authority of the Conference. The Conference is both a 10 day meeting when all decisions are made, candidates accepted for training, and ministers ordained, and the term used for 'Head Office'. Representatives, both lay and ordained, are sent from each District, for the annual 10 day Conference. Representatives are also sent from the local churches to the 'Circuit Meeting' and from the Circuit Meeting to the 'District Synod'.

When a minister is deemed ready for ordination, he/she is sent to Conference; usually after a pre-ordination retreat of several days, and 'presented to Conference', along with all the other ordinands. A vote is taken as to whether they can go forward for Ordination. This is really a formality, as all the real work on this issue is done, quietly behind the scenes, many weeks beforehand. After being accepted by the Conference, Ordination follows very quickly, usually the same day.

Bob's pre-ordination retreat was at Rydal in the Lake District. Here, he met again his college friends, and especially the members of his 'tea club' from Headingley. After 3 years together, they were very close, and delighted to be together again.

The 10 days Bob spent with us were very enjoyable. He was gone from early in the morning until late at night, and invariably lost his way on the London Underground system. He treated me in exactly the same way as my 2 older brothers did - with leg-pulling and generally disparaging remarks. I responded in kind - as I would with my brothers. On 18th June 1968, Bob was to be ordained, and he offered to get us tickets for the Ordination Service. We arrived at the Methodist Central Hall, Westminster, in time for the Presentation of the Ordinands to the Conference. Those due to be ordained had already had a group photograph taken, which Bob missed. There was too much excitement going on, and he was meeting old friends, in particular Ivan Wilson, with whom he had been so close at Cliff College, and whom he had not seen since.

After the official business, a whole group of us had tea together in the Central Hall, Bob's Mam and Dad, his sister Edna and her flat-mate, Viola, Bob's wife and a friend from the Halifax Circuit, my mother and I.

We were keen to allow ourselves plenty of time to get to Wesley's Chapel in City Road, the venue for one of several Ordination Services. There were no reserved seats, and Bob wanted to make sure that we all had a good view. In those days, before the Chapel was refurbished, the pulpit blocked the view of the Communion rail. Bob took charge, and marched us all on to a London bus, made us go upstairs to get a good view of the sights and neglected to check in which direction it was going! We ended up at Victoria Station! Eventually we arrived in City Road, still in plenty of time, in fact, we were the first to arrive - at least three quarters of an hour before the service was due to start, and no-one was there!

The service was due to begin at 7 p.m. and after 6.45 p.m. people without tickets were allowed in, to fill any spare seats. By the time the service started, Wesley's Chapel was packed almost to the ceiling! I had never ever been to such an uplifting occasion in all my life. As the first notes of the opening hymn - "The Saviour when to Heaven He rose" - thundered out, I was transported to heaven myself. I had never heard such wonderful singing before, and it set the stage for the most amazing service of worship I had ever, up until that time, attended. I was only 21 years old, and had only ever attended worship at my own average size church at South Harrow.

After the opening hymn and prayers, the Assistant Secretary of the Conference, the Rev Alan O. Barber presented to the President of Conference, the Rev E. Gordon Rupp, M.A.,D.D., the Candidates for Ordination, and a list of their names was read. Each Candidate stood as his name was called, and remained standing while passages of Scripture were read. Those recommended were: Matthew 28: 18-20, Isaiah 6: 1-8, Luke 12: 35-38, John 10: 9-16, John 21: 15-17, 2 Timothy 4: 1,2,5, Ephesians 4: 7,8,11-13; although not all were read. The President then asked the Ordinands, via a series of questions; whether they were ready to be Ordained and to serve as 'Ministers in the Church of God', the first question in my opinion, being the most important; 'Do you trust that you are inwardly moved by the Holy Spirit to take upon you this office and ministration, to serve God for the promoting of His Glory, for the preaching of His Gospel, and for the edifying of His people?' And the response 'I do so trust'. There followed a time of silent prayer.

After a hymn 'Creator Spirit, by whose aid', the Ordinands, a row at a time, knelt at the Communion rail, and the President, and other ministers, including one chosen personally by each Ordinand (Bob having chosen Rev Bernard Moss), laid their hands upon the head of each one of the Candidates, and said "Mayest thou receive the Holy Spirit for the office and work of a Christian Minister and Pastor, now committed unto thee by the imposition of our hands. And be thou a faithful Dispenser of the Word of God, and of His Holy Sacraments, in the Name of the Father and of the Son and of the Holy Ghost." Each Candidate was then presented with a Bible, with the words, "Take thou authority to fulfil the office of a Minister in the Church of Christ." When all the men had been ordained, they stood, and the President said "In the name of our Lord Jesus Christ, the only Head of the Church, I hereby declare you to be ordained to the office of the Holy Ministry". After a hymn ('Lord, if at Thy command the word of life we sow, watered by Thy almighty hand, the seed shall surely grow:') the Ministers and Ordinands received Holy Communion. The hymn 'Behold the Servant of the Lord', was followed by the Charge (sermon), given by the Ex-President of Conference, the Rev Irvonwy Morgan, M.A.,B.D.,Ph.D. The service closed with the singing of 'O Thou who camest from above' and the Blessing.

As you can imagine the service was fairly long, and there was just the briefest of time to chat, before Bob's family had to make their way to Kings Cross for trains. Bob asked Mum and me to take his parents, and Edna and Viola to the train to see them off. His wife had a later train, and they had time for some light refreshments before they said their good-byes. We met up with Bob later, and travelled back to Harrow together. Midnight found the three of us waiting for the last bus at Rayners Lane, with Bob and I singing 'O Thou who camest' to the tune 'Wilton', having sung it to 'Hereford' at the Ordination - the first time I had ever heard that tune!

Although the Ordination was for Bob the highlight of the Conference, there were still three more days of business to complete; the Ordinands were expected to be there, but Bob tried to get home on the Thursday (20th) for David's fifth birthday, but was told, at the station, that he couldn't use his train ticket until Friday afternoon! In the end, we said two lots of good-byes to him, one on Thursday, and one on Friday.

Chapter Eight

And so we went our separate ways, and got on with our lives, just keeping in very loose contact, exchanging Christmas cards etc.

For Bob, it was back to Circuit life in Halifax for what, he hoped, would be several more years, but it was not to be so.

In the August, following his ordination, Bob, learned that his marriage was over, although it was not until March 1969, that he and his wife finally separated.

In April 1969, Bob had to take Paul back to boarding school at Bath, but he had also decided that life would be intolerable if he stayed in Halifax, and so he asked if he could be moved to another Circuit. With travelling south to Kingswood School he had the opportunity to go from there to Rickmansworth to meet the officials of the Watford Circuit, with a view to moving there that summer. But the big problem was, where could he stay with John and David? And more to the point, he needed somewhere to leave them while he met the Circuit staff; somewhere that would not cost him too much money. He wrote to us to ask if we could help, and we were only too willing to do so.

They arrived fairly late in the evening, very tired, and David in particular, looking very lost and alone. Paul was there too. When it came to the crunch, he really didn't want to stay at boarding school, and Bob took him away, there and then.

They stayed with us for several days. Bob was invited to go to the Watford Circuit that September, and having sorted that out, felt able to relax for a few days. He even managed to get a dispensation from the District Synod, and was able to stay a little longer. We took them all over the place, including an exhausting day in London, and my one and only visit to the Post Office Tower, which had only recently opened.

When the Methodist Conference met in the summer of 1969, several circuits had to 'drop' a minister. Watford was one of those Circuits, and they decided it would be best for all concerned if that could be the new man going in - Bob. He was offered a place at Gateshead, on Tyneside, but Bob felt it was too close to home for that point in time, and appealed;

he was offered St Austell, and he accepted the appointment. He was to be in Pastoral charge of the Zion section of the Circuit with 7 churches. Mum and I had already planned our holiday for the first two weeks of September, but we cancelled our plans and went to St Austell to help Bob and the boys get settled. His mother-in-law had been with Bob in the last days in Halifax and moved with them. She was not in the least bit domesticated but was a great help with the boys when Bob had to be out.

The following months were a busy time for Bob. A new Circuit always is a busy time for the Minister, as he gets to know what is going on, and has the marathon task of learning hundreds of new names, and putting faces to them!

As our friendship grew and deepened, I tried to visit fairly regularly - usually about once a month, and as the New Year began, we started to make plans to get married.

We felt we should marry as soon as possible. The boys desperately needed some stability in their lives, and apart from that, our phone calls, and my visits by train were running away with any spare money we had. Bob had met with the Chairman of the District several times, and on 3rd March, my birthday, we were due to see him at his home in Truro, at 9 a.m. We awoke to a light covering of snow, and didn't think anything of it, but we didn't realise, that Cornwall sees so little snow that everything changes, no matter how light the covering. We crawled, in heavy traffic, all the way to the Chairman's house, and arrived late! All turned out well, though, and we were given permission to marry. We returned to St Austell via Mevagissey. By this time, the sun had come out, the snow was gone, and we had a beautiful walk around the harbour. After lunch at home, we dashed to Plymouth, an hour's drive away, and bought our wedding rings.

Setting the date proved more difficult. Bob was determined that the boys would not miss any school, and weekends were pretty busy, in the end, we decided on the Wednesday after Whit Sunday. All the preparations were going well, and we reached the Friday before the wedding - 22nd May. Fairly early that morning, I received a panic phone call from Bob, asking if I could put a cheque in the post for £10. Being the end of the quarter, money was low, but he had only just realised that he had no money to buy petrol to actually get to Harrow. Without that, there couldn't even be a wedding! Fortunately, in those days, the banks were open on Saturday mornings, and that day the Post Office was super efficient, delivering the letter by first post, and so the panic was over, and the Bridegroom would be able to get to the wedding after all!

Whit Monday was a Bank Holiday in those days, and the schools were off for the whole week. Bob, the boys and their Grandma came up to us on the Bank Holiday Monday; a journey which normally took all day, and with the Bank Holiday traffic, it was even longer. They arrived, tired, hot and sticky, worn out and hungry, and Bob and I, at least, were glad that it would be the last time either of us had to cope, in that way, alone; in future we would do it together.

Tuesday was a hectic day, getting everything sorted out. Bob's parents arrived, and other friends too, and they all had to be taken to the friends' houses where they were to stay. Bob spent the night with the Best Man and his family. Mervyn and Daisy Brown were from the North East. They and Bob had instantly hit it off, and he was the automatic choice to be with Bob at our wedding. In the end, Bob got the best deal because life was chaotic at my home.

Edna and Viola arrived very early on the wedding morning, and I was only just about up. My nieces, Karen and Amanda arrived at 8 a.m. for me to do their hair, which was followed by my lifelong friend, Margaret, also a hairdresser, arriving to do my hair. After that, friends arrived to wish me well, and the photographer was with us by 10 a.m. And so, at 11 a.m. on 27th May 1970, we were married. It was a glorious day, in fact, baking hot, as it had been for many weeks beforehand - Bob was so intent on getting a tan, that he had worked outside whenever he could, but he overdid it, and in the wedding photos you can only see one side of his nose, the other side had a huge scab on it! The boys had grey trousers, pale blue shirts and beige sweaters. It was far too hot for the sweaters, but they refused to take them off and Paul was physically sick with heat and also the emotion of the occasion.

Not being able to afford to stay anywhere overnight, we had decided to drive back to St Austell that afternoon. We eventually said our farewells at about 4.30 p.m. but the boys, who were staying with Mum for a few days, were more excited about an evening trip to London, and also Heathrow Airport with Mervyn Brown!

Before we finally left the Harrow area, we called at the cemetery, and I laid my bouquet on my Father's grave. Bob left his buttonhole there too.

We also tried to get the 'graffiti' off the car - my youth fellowship had written 'Just Married' etc. all over it in white shoe cleaner, and stuck rose petal confetti on to it. In the sun it had baked on hard. We got some of it off, but still drove to Cornwall with white film all over the dark green car.

We took no food with us, expecting to buy something on the way, but we hadn't realised that Wednesday was early closing day, and nowhere was open. We eventually found a fish and chip shop in Wincanton. By the time we got to Exeter, it was almost 10 p.m. and the fog came down. We were tired, and Bob, being the only driver, was exhausted, and so, to keep awake, we sang every hymn and chorus that we could think of, all the way to St Austell. We eventually went indoors just after midnight.

Bob had not really taken any time off, and was officially on duty the next day, but we did manage a short lie-in. Once we were up, he went off to collect Cindy, the puppy that he had bought a couple of months before, from the kennels. While he was gone, a very irate, elderly Methodist Local Preacher arrived at the front door with a problem that at the time, I didn't know anything about, nor did I understand it. In the end, I told him that I didn't know or understand what he was talking about as I had only been married the day before! He stopped dead, and went off, agreeing to contact Bob later. This was a rather unfortunate introduction to life as a Minister's wife. As if that wasn't enough for one day, we had to be at the village of Trethurgy that afternoon, to judge various classes in their village show, but we had to clean the car before we could go, and that seemed to be an endless job.

The following Sunday, the boys and their Grandma arrived home, by train, from London. The rail trip gave them as much excitement as actually seeing their Dad again, and, all in all, I think they had enjoyed their week away. Monday morning saw them back at school, and for them, the familiar routine.

For Bob and I there was to be a honeymoon – if you could call it that! Bob had seen an advertisement for a Christian hotel on the outskirts of Newquay. It was only half an hour's drive away from St Austell, so there were no heavy travelling expenses, and only supposed to be a stone's throw from the sea, which it was, if you dropped the stone over the edge of some extremely high cliffs - otherwise it was inaccessible! The hotel itself was relatively comfortable, but the owners were fundamentalist Christians who ran a very strict regime - we even had to ask permission to stay out late, when we went into Newquay to see the film 'Oliver'.

When it came to payment, any cheques had to be paid several days before you left in order to have them cleared by the bank before your departure. Methodist Ministers are paid quarterly, on the first day of September, December, March and June. We had left St Austell on Monday, 1st June, before we had received our stipend, and so, on the Wednesday, we had to go back to the Superintendent Minister in St Austell, Rev Leonard Race, to collect our cheque and pay it into the bank, before we could pay the hotel for our stay there! By the Friday, we had had enough, and, instead of returning home late afternoon as planned, we left straight after breakfast.

Within two weeks of our wedding, Bob was extremely ill. He had had several bouts of stomach pain over the previous months, but put it down to indigestion; this time though, he was really poorly, and I sent for the doctor. He was ordered to bed, and told not to get up for anything, but for Bob, this was impossible, he needed to know what was going on - especially with a new wife let loose in the house! For me, it was a frightening experience, and the fact that Bob kept getting up for any excuse he could think of, frightened me even more, and on one occasion, he was out of bed, 'supervising' David's bath, when the doctor called, unexpectedly. I called to him, but Dr Phillips was one jump ahead of me, and yelled "Get back into bed, Bob, the doctor's here!"

After about two weeks, everything settled down, and it was decided that it was caused by stress, and so Bob was given a mild tranquilizer to take when he was coping with difficult problems. These did help, but he was to suffer with this increasing problem for the next seven years, until the doctors at last got to the bottom of it.

Life began to settle down, and we had a beautiful summer. Bob's mother-in-law, eventually left us at the beginning of the school summer holidays, and went back to her home town of Ashington, North-umberland. Bob's parents came for two weeks during the school holidays, bringing Bob's nephew with them, and they were followed by many others; this set the pattern for much of our married life. Although we were not able to get away very often - during term time we were tied with the children, and Bob was tied up at weekends - we loved having visitors.

My mother, of course, was a regular visitor, and she remembered one of those early visits. We were all seated round the dinner table, and as we started our meal, she too picked up her knife and fork, only to discover that Bob had tied the knife, fork and spoon together with thin cotton; as she picked them up, all three shot in the air! This was typical of Bob, and life with him, I quickly discovered, was never dull.

Another abiding memory of our time in St Austell is the visit of Prince Charles. He was due to arrive at the railway station, and from there, he would travel by car. The railway station was a very short walk from our house; that is if you took the short cut through the disused cemetery, which is now [as it was then] transformed into a park.

Bob always made a big thing about not being in favour of royalty in general, but on this occasion, he used David, who was about eight at the time, as his excuse. I was told that David wanted to see Prince Charles, and so Bob would be taking him to the station. When they arrived back home, they had not only joined the crowd at the railway station, but run back through to the other end of our road, because they didn't get a good enough view the first time! All this on the pretext that David was desperate to see the Prince!

Chapter Nine

Throughout the winter of 1970/1971, the District Redevelopment Committee spent every Saturday in the St Austell Circuit. The Circuit Meeting had requested that a report be prepared, to help them to decide on the best way forward for the Circuit as a whole. There were 37 churches in the Circuit, and every Saturday afternoon one church was visited; the members met with the commitee, and copious notes were taken. At the end of this long process, the report was sent to the Superintendent Minister, and its conclusions were, that 21 of the 37 churches should close, and the work be concentrated in the remaining 16.

At the outset, the Super, Len Race, had pointed out, that if the committee were going to put all that work in, the Circuit must be prepared to carry out its suggestions. Everyone wholeheartedly agreed. When the report was presented, members of the Circuit Meeting were horrified. A special, open meeting of the Circuit was called, and St John's Methodist Church in St Austell, was packed to overflowing. I sat with Bob and the other Circuit Ministers. The meeting started calmly enough, with the singing of the hymn 'This, this is the God we adore', followed by an opening prayer by the Superintendent Minister, who was in the chair, after that chaos erupted, with everyone trying to have their say, and to persuade the meeting that their ideas were the best ones. Sadly, very few people suggested that we should seek to learn what God's will was for the future of the Circuit.

From the very moment that he arrived in the St Austell Circuit, Bob struck up a friendship with a young couple who were members at Bridge Chapel, one of Bob's section. Sallie and Arthur Roberts supported him while he was there without me; they supported and loved us both throughout our courtship and have been there for us throughout our marriage. Sadly, Sallie died a few years ago, but the friendship continues with Arthur, who is loving, caring and supportive of every member of the family.

It was to Sallie and Arthur we turned after that meeting, as did several others of the Circuit staff. It was not a happy time for the Circuit, and the staff felt really isolated.

Within a week of that meeting taking place, a letter arrived from Watford. It was from the Senior Circuit Steward, writing on behalf of the Circuit, informing us that three of the Circuit staff would be leaving in the summer of 1972, and would we be interested in going to the North Watford section of the Circuit. Had things been going well in St Austell, I don't honestly think that we would have considered it, after all, the boys had had enough upheaval, now was a time to settle and adjust and build ourselves up, both as individuals and as a family. However, we were still recovering from all the Circuit trauma and we talked about our future. Paul was, by this time, 14 years old, and although the move would be at a difficult time for him, we felt that, academically, he could cope with it, and the bonus was that, in the London area, he would be able to choose whatever career he wanted. In St Austell, in those days, there was virtually nothing except the China Clay industry. And, in the end, that was the deciding factor. The house would be a bit small, but it did have central heating, it would be a welcome change from the cold, draughty manse in St Austell.

Around about the time that all this was going on, the decision was made, that my mother should come to live with us. She had been very lonely since I had left home, not only had I gone, but all my hairdressing clients stopped at the same time, and it left a tremendous hole in her life that she found hard to fill.

It was Bob who first suggested she should come, he felt that I was rushed off my feet caring for the large house and him and the boys, and that Mum was finding life unbearable with too little to do. It seemed the ideal solution, added to which, we knew that, in just over a year's time, we would be going to Watford, and if it didn't work out, she could look for a small place of her own then. As it turned out, between May 1971 and August 1972, the price of houses rocketed, and Mum's house, which was sold for round about £6,000 in 1971 would have been selling at £23,000 in 1972; she no longer had enough money to buy any property at all. Whether she should have put it on the rental market initially rather than sell it, is the obvious question to ask with hindsight, but we left it up to her to make all the decisions, and to do what she wanted. The outcome, of course, was that she stayed with us until her death in 1994, 11 months after Bob, and I have to believe that that was how God wanted it to be.

And so we settled down for the rest of our time in Cornwall. Before long we were delighted to discover that I was expecting our first child.

Rachael Melanie Wilson arrived in the early hours of 15th February 1972, weighing 8 lbs. exactly. I was told that she was extremely overdue and I should have had her a month earlier, when both she and I would have coped far better with the birth!

The boys received her very well. In those days, it was quite an embarrassment to have a baby in the family when you were nearly 15, and Paul coped very well. David found life a little difficult having suddenly been ousted from his position as baby of the family, and for a while it was a bit of a love/hate relationship. John, however, adored her. Almost every photo we have with the children together, John is holding her, and even today, there is still a special bond between them.

Bob, of course, was delighted to have a little girl, in fact, when he took me to Penrice Hospital, when I was in labour, he joked to me, "And if it's another boy, don't come home!" Rachael was a very placid baby, and we hardly knew we had her for the first months in St Austell. We did have a few problems with her sleeping at about six weeks, but afterwards it wasn't too bad. When we moved, things changed, and she didn't sleep properly again until she was 3 years old!

The time from Rachael's birth until it was time to leave St Austell simply flew by, and it's true to say, that we never did appreciate the fact that we only lived a mile from the sea until after it was gone.

Chapter Ten

We had a warm welcome in Watford. Three 'new' Ministers all arrived together, which must have been a nightmare at times, for those on the receiving end. As one of the newcomers was the Superintendent Rev Arthur Ayre, our welcome service was held in his main church, Trinity, at 7pm on Saturday September 2nd. Rev F. Barrie Heafford made up the trio. Arthur had 2 churches in the centre of the town, Trinity and Vicarage Road (just a few yards from the football ground). Barrie had Bushey and Oxhey, and Bushey Heath. Bob should have had St Albans Road and Harebreaks, but they came together shortly before we arrived, and worshipped, (and everything else) at the Harebreaks site, changing its name to North Watford Methodist Church. The St Albans Road premises were later sold to another denomination.

Already in the Circuit were W. L. Vaughan Tong, who had pastoral charge of Rickmansworth, Croxley Green and Berry Lane (Rickmansworth), and W. John Crocker, who had Kings Langley, Abbots Langley and Carpenders Park. The Circuit staff got on extremely well together, and there are many happy memories of Christmas parties and summer 'get-togethers' in the garden at John's Manse in Abbots Langley. The summer meetings were always the five Ministers and their wives, but the Christmas parties were thrown open to all the Methodist Ministers and their wives who lived in the area. Rev Richard L. J. Kaye (Jack) and Mary always came. He was Chairman of the London North West District, and lived in Watford, as did various Ministers appointed to posts in London: Alan Birtwhistle and Gordon Shaw spring to mind. Also, several Supernumeraries (retired Ministers) lived in the Circuit, and they came too: Noel Brewis being there throughout our time in Watford, and also Len White.

Circuit Staff meetings were obviously a great deal of fun. All the Ministers had a great sense of humour, and Bob came home chuckling, many a time, after someone had told a very funny joke.

The Watford Circuit was a new beginning for us. It was the first Circuit in which we arrived together, and it made such a difference. I saw my role as a 'backroom' girl, supporting Bob in everything he did, going to functions with him when necessary, but mainly making sure that our home life was stable and running smoothly. This suited me down to the ground, because I was terrified of doing anything at all in public! I remember disliking meetings where Bob was drawn away in conversation with others, because I hated being left alone. I would try to get out of going, but he always insisted, and promised that this time he would stay by my side constantly, but he never did!

The people of North Watford were very friendly and welcoming, and we soon began to feel at home. The boys settled at their new schools, and we enjoyed our first warm winter for several years thanks to the central heating. The Manse was a Thirties semi-detached house with bay windows; it consisted of two double bedrooms and two box rooms, and I look back and wonder how we ever coped, but cope we did, and it seemed fine at the time, The loft was boarded for us which gave us an enormous amount of storage room and that helped considerably. The downside was that it was situated on a busy road, so we had to watch Rachael if ever she was in the front garden with us. In fact we did have one very scary moment when she was about two.

Bob was working on the back garden on a cold winter's day; I was upstairs, dusting, in our bedroom, which overlooked the front garden. As I looked out of the window, I saw a toddler walking up the road, entirely on her own. It took a few seconds for it to register that the little girl was wearing the same coat and hat as Rachael had; and another few seconds to realise it actually was Rachael!! She had let herself out of the garden while Bob was looking the other way, and was heading for the house that was next door but one; the boys had been feeding the neighbour's cat while they were away, and had taken Rachael with them - she was off to see the cat! Bob's comment? 'Well the gate was shut; how did she get out?' It hadn't occurred to him that she was now tall enough to reach the latch!

North Watford was not an easy church by any means, but then, most churches go through difficult periods. Tom and Doris Furness were always very supportive, especially with their prayers; they wrote, "After a limited experience as a Minister, the seven years he spent at North Watford were far from easy, for as a Church it was known by Ministers as a 'hard nut to crack', and this meant for him much study and preaching."

It was a testing time for Bob, not least because he had pastoral charge over only one church, and that meant an awful lot of sermon writing. In the early days there, the decision was made to build a new hall, and there was a lot of agonising over the finance. I remember he and Arthur Ayre had to make a trip to the Home Missions Division in London to meet officials there with regard to a grant. But the fund-raising started with a vengeance, and the hall - Unity Hall to commemorate the merger of the two Churches - was officially opened in May 1975.

In Autumn of 1974 saw both Susan Sulstan and me expecting babies at Easter. Susan's husband, Peter, had taken over from Vaughan Tong at Rickmansworth and their baby was due at almost the same time as ours; theirs, if I remember rightly, was due on Easter Saturday (29th March), ours was due on Maundy Thursday (27th March). You can imagine the friendly rivalry that went on in Staff meetings. On Tuesday, 25th Arthur Ayre phoned, hardly able to hold back the laughter, as he told Bob that the Sulston's had beaten us to it, and that they had had a little girl (after 2 boys), Rachel, that morning. Bob had been hoping that our baby might be born on Easter Sunday - "the best day of the year to be born", well this just made him more desperate - "We can only top that if ours is born on Easter Day". This all may sound rather trivial and petty, but it was just good natured rivalry, and we all had a lot of fun with it. Whether the Lord joined in or not, I don't know, but Maundy Thursday came and went, so did Good Friday and Easter Saturday, when I tired myself out re-organising Rachael's bedroom. During the Saturday evening, Bob appeared with a meal he had cooked himself - steak, chips, mushrooms, tomatoes etc., and I remember quipping, "What's this, the prisoner's last meal?"

At about twenty minutes past six on Easter Sunday morning, I woke with a pain; I dug Bob in the ribs and told him to check the time as I thought this was it. The next one was seven minutes later, followed by another, 5 minutes later. By then, I was out of bed getting myself organised. The policy at that time was to ring the ambulance station; if there was not a vehicle available we would be told what to do. We had to ring when the contractions were about twenty minutes apart. I was ready for off, but I couldn't get Bob motivated at all. He had some cereal, then he thought he would have a shave! When told to hurry, he said "We can't do anything until the contractions are twenty minutes apart". He moved rather quickly when told that we were way beyond that stage!

We had our first snow for 3 years on Good Friday, and so, it was the first snow that Rachael had ever seen, and we couldn't keep her in. The boys, particularly David, made snowmen, played snowballs and generally gave her a wonderful time. When I went to her room to tell her that I was going to the hospital to get the new baby, all she wanted to know was "Has it been snowing?" Well, the answer was 'yes' - it was an absolute blizzard, and I was so pleased to be in the ambulance - Bob followed in the car. At first, they thought that the baby would arrive before Bob had to leave for his morning service, but things slowed down, and he left us at about 9.30 a.m. Let Bob tell the rest of the story, as he used it at a Women's Meeting, entitled "Personal Experience of Shrodells Maternity Hospital".

Easter Sunday, just after 6 a.m., my wife woke saying she had pains, could I time the intervals (about every 6-7 minutes). Well, I read in some Medical Text Book about the pains being every 20 minutes, and I thought I had time to shave and have breakfast before it was time for the ambulance to take my wife to hospital. It wasn't until my wife and mother-in-law began to shout at me, that I got the message. On the radio, some days after, someone else had a similar experience, and in the night, the wife tried to get her husband moving, "We're under starter's orders", she said. His reply, "Come back to bed, it'll probably wear off".

When I left hospital, just before 10 a.m., a Methodist midwife, and a Methodist Sister were in attendance. I had missed my marmalade and toast early on, so I came home, got shaved and ready for Church, had two slices of toast and marmalade, and then had to conduct the Morning Service followed by Holy Communion. I rang the hospital as soon as I got home as I wanted to be there for the birth. Sister said "If you come now you may be lucky". That was twenty minutes to 1p.m. Our daughter was born at 12.44 p.m. so I missed the actual birth only by minutes." (Sarah Michelle was born on March 30th 1975, and weighed 7lb.12oz.)

I was only in hospital until the Wednesday, and only a couple of days later Jack Kaye, the Chairman of District, and Mary, his wife came to visit us. Bob says:-

While they were here, there was a telephone call from the box outside the Church. A man wanted his fare to Preston. His opening words were "I'm a Methodist, and must get back to Lancashire, my Father is dangerously ill." How would you deal with that situation?

The Chairman said he had become hardened to that kind of appeal, and I'm afraid I am getting that way, after being taken in so many times in the past. However, the telephone caller couldn't be put off, and came round to the Manse. A real man of the road; about 45, bearded, strong shoes, knapsack, even road maps. He got rather awkward when I said I couldn't really give him the cost of his fare, and eventually he went away grumbling to himself, and then, shouting to me, "There's only one thing left to do, I'll throw myself under an express train", although I must confess that I had to laugh, for he went in the opposite direction. However, two days later, on the front page of the Echo (Watford) "Body found on railway line". Thankfully, it wasn't the chap who had called to see me.

Poor Bob was really harassed that week, and only a few days later I had a bad attack of cystitis, and the doctor had to be called out late at night. He reported to the Women's Meeting "I got the job of feeding Sarah at about 5 a.m.!"

During the winter I was expecting Sarah, the building work was going on for Unity Hall, and so, it worked out very well that it was to have a grand opening, with a guest preacher, in the middle of May, and Bob was able to have a morning free to be 'Dad' for Sarah's baptism. When Rachael was born, it meant a day off, and baptism at Mevagissey, another section of the Circuit.

The joy of Sarah's baptism was, all too soon, marred by Paul's sudden decision to go to live with his mother, her husband and young son, in Halifax. Paul was, by now, 18 years old and able to make his own decisions. For Bob and me, it was devastating news; Bob managed to keep his emotions under control, but I went to pieces. I found it hard to accept that after five difficult years of adjustment, he was leaving, and within days. I well remember Bob doing some straight talking to me, and finishing up with, "We either smile and wave him off happily, and he'll be back, or we make a fuss, and never see him again." It was a fortunate coincidence, that a friend of ours was travelling north, and took Paul most of the way, and we were able to wave him off from home, but as soon as they were out of sight the flood gates opened, and I cried and cried.

From the age of 21, I had suffered from depression, and, in fact, had to give up work for a while, because of a breakdown. After Rachael's birth I had been very low in spirits, but after Sarah's I really hit rock bottom. Throughout all this, Bob was a tower of strength, although, at times, I know I pushed him to the limits, but by the time Sarah was six months old, even he had had enough. A friend recommended Dr Percy Backus, an eminent psychiatrist, and Past Vice-president of the Methodist Conference. Although he had been long retired, and was in his eighties, he still saw one or two people at his home. After one meeting, he told me, "I know what is wrong with you, and I can cure you." Then began a three year long course of tablets and blood tests. At my worst moments, I doubted the existence of God, and had stopped praying, but as my health improved, the desire to pray returned, and directly from that came the call to preach.

Bob coped through all this, and after Sarah's birth, and five years of marriage, we came out the other end, battered and bruised, but still together, and from that moment, our love deepened and grew, and went from strength to strength, until Bob's death, and beyond.

With our family complete, we settled down to the Circuit routine once more. We missed Paul terribly, but he phoned regularly, and we looked forward to that. John left school, and began work, initially in the local Waitrose, before finally moving to Chesham, and finding his niche within the building trade. As long as he was at home, we had a constant stream of girl friends who appeared at the front door with great regularity. John has also inherited Bob's knack for falling asleep anywhere. I remember one evening when the telephone rang; we had to wake him to take the call; he left the room, and a few moments later, we heard the front door close. John walked back into the room in a dazed state saying: "There's no-one there!" We had to turn him around, and push him back into the hall where the phone was.

Of course, as time went by, we had the usual ups and downs of family life; when Sarah was 11 months old, she frightened us all to death, not least my very experienced and totally capable mother. At breakfast time one morning, she had a convulsion, and once again I was in an ambulance being rushed to the Children's Ward of Watford General Hospital at Shrodells. She was in hospital for almost a week, and I think we were more traumatized by the experience than she was, but what a relief to have her home. For several years we had to watch her when she got very hot, but otherwise, there was no recurrence.

Believe it or not, within 3 months, we were back in the Accident & Emergency Department of Watford General Hospital. Rachael had spotted Sarah eating the berries of a 'Winter Cherry' house plant! Fortunately she had not eaten enough to cause any problems, but Bob always managed to get a lot of mileage out of these experiences, and used them as sermon illustrations!

It was about this time that Bob decided that he would like to wear a cassock for preaching; but the problem was the cost. It was also about this time that members and friends, Jeanette and Paul Spencer, were wanting the foundations dug for a garage; Bob offered to do it in his spare time, and between them, the cassock was bought.

Paul and Jeanette were good friends, and we all remember, very clearly, the night when, after a meeting at the church, it was agreed that they should come back to the Manse for coffee. Jeannette, Paul and I arrived back soon after 9pm, but Bob wanted to visit someone, so we agreed that he would follow a bit later. At 10.45pm, the Spencers left - Paul had to catch an early flight the next morning, but as they left, he told me to ring if I was worried, and that he should be up until about 11.30pm.

At 11.45pm, with still no sign of Bob, I phoned them. Paul immediately got dressed, and went out to look for Bob. He found him walking home along the main road. When Paul drew alongside him, Bob turned in surprise and said: "Hello Paul, what are you doing here?" Paul's response? "I'm looking for you!" Bob never lived that one down.

Chapter Eleven

Much to my disgust, Bob was required to go on a 'Further Training' course, 10 years after he left College. He managed to put it off in 1975 and 1976, because of all that was happening at home, but in the end, they caught up with him! In January 1977, he was sent to 'Lindors', the Methodist Guild Holiday Home in the Forest of Dean, Gloucestershire. Not knowing much about the area, he travelled by train from Watford Junction - the problem was that everyone else thought the same, and they were confined to the House and local countryside, unable to go very far during their leisure time.

Little did I appreciate at the time, that this 10 day break was to prepare me for events later in the year, and the Lord, as usual, prepared me every step of the way.

Bob had suddenly developed a hernia, and the hospital decided to operate at the beginning of May. The pain he had experienced within two weeks of our marriage had come and gone over the years, and we had got used to it. At times it hit him at the most inopportune moments, but we coped, with tranquilizers and gallons of thick, white, chalky medicine. The hernia operation went well and Bob was due home on the Saturday, but when I arrived at the hospital on the Friday afternoon, he was doubled up in pain. By the evening it had eased a little, but not gone, and so the doctors decided to keep him in. Saturday saw virtually no improvement, and, Sunday morning Bob phoned to tell me not to visit him that day because he was having tests. That really frightened me, because I knew it must be urgent if they were doing tests on a Sunday. The tests showed that he had Pancreatitis - inflammation of the pancreas and an extremely serious complaint. Our GP told us afterwards, that we were very fortunate that Bob was in hospital at the time. Its cause was likely to be pregnancy, alcoholism or gallstones! It was pretty obvious to everyone that Bob must have gallstones.

He was eventually in hospital for 3 weeks, being discharged on the morning of the Soccer [FA] Cup Final match - he was desperate to be home to watch the final on TV. He was given an extremely strict, fat free diet to follow, which he did, to the last detail, and told that they would have him back in 3 months time to remove the gall bladder.

On the Monday after he came out of hospital, Bob was taken in by the biggest 'con' in the whole of his ministry.

Shortly after lunch, there was a knock at the door, and my Mother went to answer it. She came back to Bob, telling him that there was a man at the front door, who wanted to talk to the Minister. Bob took him into the dining room (the study was at the Church), and was with him for several hours. When my Mother came back to me she commented that she thought she had been 'taken in' by this man, and went on to explain that a week or so before, he had called, asking for the Minister. Not liking to give too much information away, she told him that the Minister wasn't available, and she didn't know when he would be - she was just the baby-sitter!

He had chatted to her, and given her such a heart-rending story, that she had tried to contact Arthur Ayre; when he was unavailable, she asked our neighbour next-door-but-one, Rev Trevor Davies, a Baptist Minister - if he would speak to him, which he did, and Mum saw no more of him. However, when she opened the front door to him that Monday, he appeared to be very surprised to see her, in fact, quite taken aback, and Mum felt that he was trying to make contact with the Minister, not expecting to see her. By the time all this came out, it was too late to say anything to Bob, and he spent all that time with him, oblivious to our suspicions.

When the man left, we discovered that he had given Bob a slightly different story to the one he had given Mum; I can't remember all the details now, but he said he had a brain tumour, and had to make a very difficult decision about an operation, but he needed to get home to his family, hundreds of miles away, to see them before he made the decision. He had no money for the fare. He even asked if he could smoke, because he was unable to when he was alone, in case he blacked out, and set himself alight! Bob fell for it, gave him his fare, and off he went. On the Wednesday afternoon, Arthur Ayre came to visit Bob. Just as he was leaving he casually said, "By the way, I don't expect it will affect you, but there's a con man doing the rounds!" It didn't take long before Bob realised that it was the same man. "You're too late," he said, "He's been, and I gave him his fare." When Bob told Trevor Davies, his comment was "Well, he had £8 and a shirt from me, and he earned that by his acting ability!!" Believe it or not, just over two years later, he was back again. We had a house full of friends, and were enjoying some time together before we moved - we were due to leave

Watford two weeks later. This time, he got short shrift, Bob told him "you conned me once before, and you'll not do it again." He replied that he didn't want any money; he just wanted to talk to someone (the same line that he had used 2 years before). Bob's response was "Well, we have a house full at the moment, and I've nowhere to take you. If you want to talk, come back tomorrow." He never returned. Perhaps he knew the Methodist system well enough to take a chance that we had gone, and the new man was already in, but, in any case, we never saw him again.

But, back to 1977: After a few weeks convalescence, Bob was back at work. He stuck religiously to his diet, and was extremely fit, and feeling good when, on September 1st, he received the expected letter from Watford General Hospital. He went in for his operation within a few days, and it was 100% successful. He was in hospital for another 3 weeks and after further recuperation at home, he went back to work at the beginning of November.

During the long, hot summer of 1976, Barrie and Margaret Heafford, had taken part in an exchange of pastorates, and spent 6 weeks in Winchester, Virginia, U.S.A. Jim and Emily Boice and their two children, came to Bushey. We got on with them extremely well, and by the time they left, we were full of enthusiasm to do an exchange ourselves. We set the ball in motion, and were in correspondence with a minister in Michigan, when he pulled out, unexpectedly, in March 1977. At that late stage there were no exchange partners available, so we were put at the top of the list for 1978. It turned out to be a blessing in disguise; because there is no way that we would have been able to go, with Bob's health problems that year.

In the late autumn, we received the news that we had been paired with the Rev Norman Holcomb and family who lived in Emory, Virginia, which is part of the Holston Conference of the United Methodist Church. Whereas in Britain we all belong to the British Conference, the United States is so large, that there are many Conferences; although they do all meet together every four years at General Conference. All through the winter and spring, we corresponded, and made our plans for the trip. I spent months making clothes for everyone - including Bob and David! As the day drew nearer, when we would leave Watford for six weeks, we grew more and more excited, but with only a month to go we had an urgent message from Norman. Conference had met, and he was being moved to Etowah, Tennessee. They would like to go ahead with the exchange if we were happy to. At that stage, we felt that it was too late to drop out, we had made so many plans, so we said we would carry on. There was a lot of correspondence flying between Watford and Virginia for the next few weeks. About a week before we were due to leave, Mum went to Norfolk to stay with her old friend, Mrs Watson, my close friend, Margaret's mother. She had decided not to go with us as her 99 year old father was not well, and she didn't want to be too far away. John decided not to go either, and he stayed with friends in Chesham, Buckinghamshire, near to where he was working.

Chapter Twelve

Early in the morning on Tuesday, June 20th 1978, David's 15th birthday, we left our home in Watford, utterly exhausted after weeks of cleaning, and all the last minute jobs that had to be done. We were driven to Heathrow Airport by a church member, Keith Bass, who, with his wife, Kath, were to become close friends as the years went by.

Bob was the only one of us who had ever flown before, and that was 20 years before on a propeller driven plane that carried a small number of passengers. The flight from Aberdeen to Shetland - to visit Don and Mary - had been extremely rough and had left Bob with some bad memories. In those days, the stewardess gave out barley sugar sweets, and Bob made sure that in 1978, we too had a plentiful supply! In fact, he was so nervous, that he lined us all up, in the Airport Lounge, and tried to force us all to take travel sickness tablets! Some of us managed to get out of that one! In the event, the flight was very smooth, with virtually no turbulence, and we all enjoyed it immensely.

On arrival at Kennedy Airport, New York, we knew that we had a long wait for our next flight, but decided to make sure we were in the right place before we settled ourselves down.

We had flown by British Airways to New York, but the rest of the way was by Delta. The Delta Terminal was approximately 2 miles away, and so we piled into a famous New York Yellow taxi. We felt the cost was exorbitant for the distance covered, but it did save us a lot of hassle. We had landed from England at 1.40 p.m. local time, but our next flight was at 5.10 p.m., even though it had taken time to get through Customs, and to change terminals, we still had several hours to wait. Changing terminals was, in fact, a bad move, because there was nothing there to amuse the adults, let alone the children. If we looked at the TV screen to see if our flight was boarding, once, we looked at it a thousand times. Sarah was only three and Rachael six, so they took some entertaining.

Eventually, 5.10 p.m. arrived and we took off. Bob and David were delighted to be given a second, huge meal, and the girls and I enjoyed it, too. Delta treated us like royalty, and we found their service even better than British Airways.

At Chattanooga, famous for the "Choo-Choo", we had to change planes. New York was warm, when compared with London, but it was well over 70 degrees when we left, which is quite warm enough for most of us, and the contrast didn't seem <u>too</u> great. Chattanooga was a totally different story. We left a beautifully air-conditions plane, and stepped into an oven!! Even in the early evening (about 7 - 7.30 p.m.) the temperature was high in the 90's. Fortunately, a helpful airport official in New York had checked our luggage right through to Knoxville, our final destination; we were so naive that we didn't even know you could do that! Without having to chase around to find the "luggage claim" area, we were able to wait for our flight to Knoxville feeling relaxed and relieved that we were almost there. After about an hour's wait, we were on our way again, this time it was only a one hour flight, of which Sarah slept for at least 45 minutes. By the time we were ready to leave the plane, she was beyond waking, after all, it was well after 2 a.m. British time!

Knoxville is a tiny airport, and we walked off the plane straight into the arms of a minister, (resplendent in 'dog-collar") and his wife, we assumed that they were Norman and Beth Holcomb, and they were!! Within minutes, we were in their Chevrolet van (minibus), and on our way - only to stop 10 minutes later in order to get something to eat (strawberry pie and ice cream). There we were, at 10 p.m., in the dark, feeling hotter than we had ever felt at any time at home!

Over the meal, the Holcombs explained to us that there had been a change of plan. We knew that they were not moving house until the Thursday, but assumed that we would be staying in Knoxville with Beth's mother, as we had been told. However, that was not possible, so they were driving us back to Emory, where we would stay in rooms at the College where Norman had been Chaplain. The drive took another 3 hours, David and the girls slept, Bob and I tried to keep the conversation going, but kept nodding off - often in the middle of a sentence!

Breakfast, the next morning, was in the College dining hall, and consisted of scrambled eggs, sausage, pancakes and maple syrup and butter - a totally new experience, which we loved. We spent the day visiting places of interest. The two churches we would have served in, and also a local cemetery, which contained 206 unmarked graves of Confederate soldiers. It brought the message home to Bob and me, rather abruptly, that the American Civil War had only happened just over 100 years before.

Thursday, was moving day. After a 7 a.m. breakfast, again in the College dining hall, we finished loading the van, the Holcombs' tiny Honda car, and we began our journey to Etowah, a town of 6,000 people situated between Knoxville and Chattanooga. Norman drove a large removal van, Bob the Chevrolet, and Beth the Honda. Bob and Beth kept in touch by CB radio, another "first experience" for us, and a great novelty to David and Bob in the van. Beth and I had all the girls - Cindy (approx.13 years) and Brooke (4 years), and Rachael and Sarah. Rocky and Matthew were with Bob. We enjoyed our first experience of McDonalds when we stopped for lunch in Knoxville, and then, an hour later, arrived at the Parsonage in Etowah. We spent the rest of the day unpacking before the Holcombs left at 1 a.m. to spend the night with friends in Chattanooga. They left for Britain the next morning, arriving on the coldest June day for 100 years! Talking of weather, Bob noted in the diary he kept of the exchange, that at 7.45 p.m. on that Thursday night, the temperature was 86°F, at 8.45 p.m., after a thunderstorm, it was 63°F. Quite a change!

The Parsonage seemed to all of us to be luxury itself. It was situated in a third of an acre of grassland, and all the most up-to-date appliances that came with it. Washing machines etc. were all provided with the house, and it was air conditioned! The garbage disposal unit in the sink, terrified us, and we gave up using it after awhile, because it kept "stalling" on us. However, as we came to leave Etowah, to return to England, we realised its value. David carried some sacks of rubbish out to the road to be collected, and one burst open. It was crawling with maggots! We realised immediately the value of waste disposal units, even if they are terrifying!

The Exchange was a wonderful experience. We loved being in a small town in the South, deep in Indian country - Cherokee - (Etowah is the Indian word for Muddy Waters), and the love and hospitality that was showered upon us was absolutely amazing. Friendships were made that have lasted right up to the present time, and we found the South to have a character of its own, that we really loved and enjoyed.

Wednesday, 2nd August 1978, came all too soon and in the end, we ran out of time, and were unable to do all the things we would have liked to have done. We had been given so many gifts, that we bought one suitcase, and were given three more - word had spread around the Church that we needed extra luggage, and suitcases appeared on the doorstep! We were totally overwhelmed with kindness in every way, and we all shed a few tears as we said our good-byes.

Two sets of friends took us to Knoxville airport, two cars - there was no way that we could get both us and the luggage into one - drove in convoy, and we arrived in plenty of time to have a snack together. We ate strawberry pie and ice cream again, the last meal, by coincidence, the same as the first.

After photographs with Kathleen Watson and her sister, Irene, we said our goodbyes to them, but Matney and Mildred Reed stayed until our plane was out of sight, and I can still recall the picture of Mildred's red dress pressed against a window in the terminal. Rachael cried almost all the way to Chattanooga. This time we didn't need to change planes, and we just remained in our seats, on the tarmac for a few minutes while some passengers got off and others got on.

We were late arriving at J.F.K. Airport, New York, but that was to our advantage, as it meant less time to keep the girls amused. Fortunately our luggage had been booked directly through to Heathrow from Knoxville, so we had no worries about that, and having landed at 5.40 p.m. we made our way to the B.A. Departures building, and settled ourselves down to wait to be called for our 10 p.m. flight to London. We boarded at 9.30 p.m., so the wait didn't seem to be too bad.

Bob kept a diary, on behalf of the whole family, beginning from the time we got up on 20th June and ending on our arrival at home on 3rd August. He closes it by saying,

> We arrived home about 12 noon, tired but extremely glad to be home, but profoundly thankful for the experience of the past six weeks, and the generosity of the American people.

> Praise God from whom all blessings flow,
> Praise Him all creatures here below.
> Praise Him above ye heavenly host,
> Praise Father, Son and Holy Ghost.

I couldn't improve on that.

Many memories remain of that trip, far too many to retell here, but let me mention one or two.

Water-melons are extremely plentiful, and very cheap, and we were often invited to someone's home to share one with them. Although we had eaten water-melon in England, we had never seen them as big as we did in America. They were enormous, and the children loved them, but we soon learned that if we ate one too late in the evening, we were in the bathroom several times during the night. Water-melons are named that for a reason!

The kindness of a family who realised how much I admired the traditional American patch-work quilt, but couldn't afford to buy one. Viola Watson gave me one that had been made by her mother in the "Double Wedding Ring" design, almost 40 years before, which we have always treasured.

The fascination of Gatlinburg, Tennessee, a real tourist town, nestled at the foot of the Great Smokey Mountains, that could have been found anywhere in the Alps. It was the only place that we found to buy souvenirs to take home to friends. Matney and Mildred Reed took us there for the first time, and it was there that we met their daughter, Rebecca, and another lasting friendship was made. We went back on our own at a later date.

Ethel Loftis and her daughter, Debbie, who took us on a day trip to Atlanta, Georgia, leaving home before 8.00 a.m. and returning home at 1.00 a.m. - 17 hours later! Our first stop was Stone Mountain, where the figures of the 3 Confederate Generals from the Civil War, are carved into the mountainside. Robert E. Lee, "Stonewall" Jackson, and Jefferson Davis. From there, we drove through the centre of Atlanta, past the Capitol Building, with its gold dome, where the business of the State of Georgia is carried out, and past many streets and buildings named after Martin Luther King Junior. Just on the western edge of the city is an enormous amusement park named "Six Flags over Georgia". Another new experience for us. We had not seen anything as big, nor experienced an amusement park where you pay an entry fee and that is all (apart from refreshments). There was even an area where you could leave your dog, to be cared for while you were in there - in fact not only dogs – presumably anything could be left at the "Pet Park".

It cost us $8.50 to go in, and we were there for nine hours, so it was pretty good value. David had had a skateboard accident the day before, and was looking, and feeling, rather battered and bruised, but he didn't want to stay at home. Bob felt rather sorry for him - I was still rather annoyed that he had gone skate-boarding at all, when he was told not to!

- and when he wanted to go on the "Great Gasp", Bob agreed to go with him. Bob was never very good at heights, and this ride was a nightmare for him. It consisted of a seat similar to those you get on the "Big Wheel", and this was suspended from a frame with a parachute attached, all this was connected to the top of a huge pole - 200ft tall - when everyone was strapped in, the seats were hauled to the top of the pole, and let go! When the parachute slowed them right down, they were stopped and dropped again, until they reached the ground! David said that Bob shut his eyes before they were 30ft off the ground - and kept them shut until the end of the ride, saying "Just tell me when it's over!"

The other favourite was the "Log Run', now quite common over here, but new to us at that time, a sort of Roller Coaster through water; the children all loved it (as did the adults) and we went on it several times. It was the children's final choice before we left the park. The 3 hour journey home was tiring for Debbie, our driver, and she asked Bob to drive the last 70 miles home. Her car had rather strange steering, and it took Bob a while to get used to it, but not before he was stopped by the Police for swaying across the road. We were thankful we had Americans with us, who told us what to do.

It was Debbie and Ethel, who also took us to Helen, Georgia, a small town that has been turned into an Alpine village, and sells Alpine souvenirs. We had a drink in "Heidi's Tea Room", and were served by an elderly man in lederhosen!

Matney and Mildred Reed organised picnics, both for breakfast and later on in the day. They also took us to Oak Ridge, north-east of Knoxville, where the first atomic bomb was produced, and we were told that, many people in the area didn't know what they were working on until after the bomb had been dropped. Matney and Mildred opened their home to us, and treated us as family.

Kathleen Watson, her sister Irene, and also her brother J.E and his wife Viola, also took us out and about, made us ice cream, generally spoiled us, and welcomed us as long lost friends; their homes too were always open to us.

But for Bob and I, the place we enjoyed most was Lake Junaluska in North Carolina. Lake Junaluska is a Conference Centre owned by the "South Eastern Jurisdiction" of the United Methodist Church; it also has a small building on the edge of the lake, which is the Headquarters of the World Methodist Council. It is the most peaceful place we have ever been to. The Lake on a fine day is as clear as a bell, and the whole area is absolutely beautiful. It was here that we met Charles and Mary Ann Brockwell, and another lasting friendship was formed. Charles is a Methodist minister and also a Professor at Louisville University, Kentucky. We have enjoyed not only their hospitality in Louisville, but also Charles's preaching when he and Mary Ann have stayed in our home.

Since 1978, and our first 'taste' of the U.S.A., we have been convinced that the really "special something" that you experience from an exchange, rather than from a normal holiday, is the privilege of meeting people in their own homes, sharing a small part of their lives, and living in the "real" America, far away from the tourist routes and the big cities, because, after all, more people live in small towns in America than live in big cities. 20th June 1978 marked the start of a change in our lives in all sorts of ways, not least in sharing our Christian love for one another, and accepting people as they are. Bob even dared to tell jokes against the Americans - and they loved him all the more!

Chapter Thirteen

Early in 1978, we were approached by Bill Wills, a Circuit Steward in the Cheltenham Circuit, about the possibility of moving there in 1979. He worked in London at the time, and came over to see us one evening, to discuss the matter. From all he said, we felt it was worth following up, so we made arrangements to travel to Gloucestershire to have a look. On 14th February 1978, first thing in the morning, Bob, myself and Sarah set off. Sarah was not yet 3, and very reluctant to be away from both Mum and Dad at any time, let alone for a whole day! I went prepared with spare pants, spare tights, spare skirt and sweater for her, I thought I was ready for any emergency!

We had just left the Oxford by-pass and passed a sign which said "No stopping for 9 miles", when, completely out of the blue, Sarah vomited all over me! She had never ever done that before, and took us all by surprise. I asked Bob to stop, but he said he couldn't - for 9 miles! I tried to point out that this was an emergency, but he wouldn't have it, and he kept driving until we got to the Puesdown garage, only 10-15 miles from Cheltenham! I dragged Sarah into the toilet, only to find that after several freezing cold days, and snow showers, all the pipes were frozen! In the end, I did what I could, and we went on to Cheltenham. On arrival at the Super's house, where we were to meet the Circuit Staff, Joan Pile, the Super's wife, opened the door, saw our problem immediately, and took Sarah and I under her wing, helping us to get ourselves sorted out and generally freshened up. Sarah had a complete change of clothes, but I can still see myself, in a pale green suit, feeling a mess and smelling awful, for the whole day!

Having done my best with Sarah and myself, we joined the others. Wilfrid Pile, the Super, Norman Brookes from New Zealand (in England for one year), John James and John Appleby, whom we would replace. Memories are dim of that experience, but not my discomfort!

After lunch at Bill and Brenda Davis', then Circuit Steward in charge of finance, we went on to St Mark's, the largest Church in the section, and named after the area of Cheltenham, rather than the saint. Here we met the church officials, and had a rather gruelling time as they fired questions at us - Sarah fell asleep! From there we were taken on a tour of the country churches in our section, Shipton Oliffe, Andoversford, and back to the edge of the town for St Nicolas, a shared Church of England /Methodist building.

Tea was at the home of Pat and Ted Stanton (also a Circuit Steward) and their family. Here, too, we were able to relax, and their girls (junior school age and older) made a fuss of Sarah.

We returned home, feeling that Cheltenham was the right place for us to go, and that we would follow the invitation process through.

The next step was for the Circuit Stewards to hear Bob preach, and the Davis', the Wills' and the Stantons all came up to tea one Sunday, and we went on to hear Bob preach at a United Service at the local Anglican Church. They must have liked what they heard, because, very shortly afterwards, our official invitation to go to the Cheltenham Circuit arrived, and we accepted, wholeheartedly. We received several other invitations to look at Circuits while we were talking to the Cheltenham folk, but we didn't follow any of them up, believing that Cheltenham was where God was calling us to go.

From about 1976, Bob, at the urging of the Circuit Staff, had been working towards setting up an industrial chaplaincy in Watford. It was a long, time-consuming business, and involved several courses at Luton Industrial College, before he was able to even begin to take soundings in local industry. Eventually, talks at Scammells, part of British Leyland which made tank transporters, and other heavy vehicles for the armed forces, began to look promising. After some of the preliminaries, it was decided that the next step would be, to meet the Union representatives – shop stewards etc. Bob was very apprehensive about this meeting, and went in fear and trembling. For a while, it was tough going. The men were very sceptical about it all, and when they learned that it was an unpaid chaplaincy, they were totally incredulous! Why would anyone want to go into the factory for nothing! Then they felt that perhaps Bob was going to capitalise on the fact that the men on the factory floor were having to keep a close eye on their work, and couldn't escape his 'clutches', and he would then brow beat them into becoming Christians! Bob again patiently explained that he would be there to help with any problems, to get alongside people, to visit the sick etc., but only if they wanted him to, he would not intrude. Suddenly, everyone relaxed, and said, "O.K., we'll give it a try".

Because Bob had worked so hard to be allowed into the factory, he always considered it a privilege to be there, and tried not to miss the one day a week he spent with them. He always made sure that one week he ate lunch with the men from the factory floor, and the next with the 'white collar' workers. One man was violently opposed to Bob being there, and so the Personnel Manager asked Bob to steer clear of him, but within weeks, he had come round, too.

Several happy years were spent with the men at Scammells, and Bob made a lasting impression on many people. Even 12 years after we had left Watford, Bob was asked to go back to take the funeral of a man who had always admired him, even though he was not a committed Christian himself. But that feeling was mutual, because Bob received as much from his friends at Scammells, as he gave to them.

As is usual when you come to the end of an appointment, you reflect on what you have achieved; you sometimes regret that you've run out of time to do all the things you had planned. But as you look back, you also look forward to your new Circuit with a mixture of excitement and trepidation, and amongst all final farewells for every group and meeting that you have been involved with, are the personal farewells. Watford was no exception and there were many quiet get-togethers with people whom we had grown to love, as we shared our memories and our hopes for the future.

Many kind things have been said, by our friends from Watford days, about Bob. One friend described him as a "kind, gentle man, but very determined". Another said "as a minister to us, and an Ambassador of Our Lord, he was most kind, good, understanding and a good preacher, plus a very good listener to all our problems."

Jean and Frank Gardiner have remained good friends, and Bob went back to Watford to take part in their daughter, Lesley's, wedding. They remember very clearly Bob's conversion memories, but also comment, "Everyone who knew Bob, was aware of his great courage and determination, if he made up his mind to achieve something, nothing within his power would prevent him."

Jenny and George Thompson were friends of mine from Harrow, whom Bob married in 1973, and Jenny says "George and I have much to be thankful for to Bob - he was so kind to us when we got married."

Tom and Doris Furness wrote "His pastoral work was reflected in his care and kindness to many. In January 1978, in a bitterly cold, snowy spell, I (Tom) was admitted to hospital, and he took Doris every day to visit me. This is a memory of Bob which we will never forget. An elderly lady of 90, not a member of our Church, still remembers him with affection, and the occasion, when he willingly gave her transport for a well-needed holiday at the seaside.

"Bob had a very rare gift, he was a good listener, and in a quiet way, tried to enter in to the problems of others.

"Through the Brotherhood and Sisterhood Movement, we annually met some of the embers and friends from Cheltenham, who spoke highly of his long ministry there.

"When on special occasions he visited us at North Watford, Doris and I have marvelled at his sincerity and eloquence, and have been very conscious, that after his exchange with Dr N. Holcomb, and other visits to the United States, Bob's spiritual life had deepened and his ministry was more effective because of his nearer communion with His Lord."

Throughout our time in Watford, we had quite close contact with Den and Sheila Wright and family. The whole family, at that time, were heavily involved in the Scouting Movement, and were members of the local Anglican Church. Their eldest daughter, Janet and her family have become very close friends, and continually support us with their prayers. Sheila Wright says of Bob, "He had great courage, and was always such a kind, understanding man. He always gave me the feeling that he was always there, and maybe we took him for granted. The kindness he showed to Janet when she was getting married. I know she was worried, she was starting not only a new life with David [a Church Army officer], but so different to what she had been used to. On her wedding day, he spent a little time with her, and I know it helped her."

Jan herself wrote a list of comments:-

Bob, -
A good listener, and never seemed to judge,
Had time for people, a friend,
Great help to me when I needed a spiritual guide, when C. of E.
failed.

*Our Wedding - spending time before the wedding, chatting (while
you did my hair)
Many times offering prayer
Used the missing cat poster in Mum's window as part of a sermon,
The many job references he carefully wrote on my behalf
Sense of humour - never wishing to forget his roots, his
background
The camera - we both recall the use of the camera!
David remembers him being a leading light in Church Unity.*

Jan ends by saying "Joy, when I sit and think back, there have been so
many times that you and Bob have been there, I hope some of the above
helps (in the biography)."

Amongst our closest friends from North Watford days are Kath and Keith
Bass. We were not particularly close during our time there, but the
friendship has blossomed and grown as the years have gone by. Keith
vividly remembers, word for word, his first conversation, or should I say,
the opening sentences of the first conversation that he had with Bob.

Keith and Frank Gardiner led the Youth Club at that time, and Bob had
been either in the Church or the vestry. He presumably decided to visit
the Youth Club while he was there, and so he wandered from the Church
into the hall. He walked up to Keith and said "I'm Bob Wilson, how are
you? Alright?" Keith points out that the "alright?" was a favourite
expression of Bob's, I had never noticed it. He remembers that his first
impression of him was his warm, friendly attitude, and the way he
approached people would be good for the Church.

After his death, Kath Bass wrote of Bob, "One of the things that stands
out in our minds as regards Bob was the time he gave in visiting people.
We did not have to be ill or in trouble, he would just appear from time to
time. As soon as he heard of anyone who was ill, he was soon by their
bedside, talking with them, and offering prayers.

"Another thing we liked, was, if you had any problems, Bob was a willing
and intent listener. He was genuinely interested and concerned, and
one soon felt some sort of relief, by just speaking to him.

"Myself, I have the disability of not hearing well, and have to wear a
hearing aid. Bob soon realised, that I was self-conscious of the fact, and

he would make light of it, by saying, Can you hear me Kath? What wave length are we on today Radio One or Radio Four?

"Yes, Bob would put you at your ease, and he was a sympathetic and caring Minister, and we shall always remember him for his caring ways."

In the early days of 1978, Allan Flewers, a friend from my Youth Club days at South Harrow, contacted us to see if we knew of any Church members who could offer temporary accommodation, until his own place was ready. In the end he stayed with us for 3 months, leaving us immediately before we left for our exchange to Etowah. He writes: "It was a great pleasure to be part of that bustling household, composing of Grandma downwards, amongst which, Bob seemed to perform a good-natured and humorous, but slightly baffled, balancing act. He certainly made me curl up with laughter at times. Having been 'patronised' by so many Methodist Ministers before and since (often in the nicest way), Bob's easy-going and relaxed attitude was like a breath of fresh air to me. I never felt he was intent on changing human nature - his own or anyone else's, but took a realistic and pragmatic view. This appeared to affect his preaching style, which was detached, the opposite of fire and brimstone. None the worse for that; and every sermon I ever heard him preach contained something which caught my attention, and made a telling point. A quite unique Methodist Minister - being Bob Wilson, a good chap, who you could get to know, with no pretensions, and whose company you could enjoy and be relaxed in. I have liked others, and felt, as a member of a Church, the Minister should be supported totally and unequivocally, unlike many other members who seemed to want the Minister to be something more than he could possibly be! Is that the difference between Bob and the others - he just didn't care too much, and said, you must take me as I am? Anyhow, that barrier I found with others, was never apparent with Bob. My observation - although I have never discussed this subject with anyone else - leads me to suspect, almost everyone else who encountered him would agree with my view."

And so, our seven years in the Watford Circuit drew to an end, and Tuesday, 21st August saw two huge removal vans outside the Manse in Bushey Mill Lane. Loading up took nearly all day, and in fact, we were running so late, that poor Keith Bass was landed with taking several black sacks of rubbish to the Council Tip, before the new Minister moved in, because it had closed before we could get away. One of our members, Mrs Page, had kindly given us a huge meal at lunchtime - we went in relays - and another friend gave us tea before we went on our way. Jeanette Spencer had been ready for us for ages, but we were so late, that we rushed through our food, and were on the road within half-an-hour.

Six of us were wedged into our medium sized saloon car. Grandma had Sarah on her knee (this was before the dangers of riding without seat belts in the back of cars was realised), and David and Rachael sat with the budgie, Smoky, in his cage, across their laps. Bob drove, and I had the dog, Snowy, a West Highland Terrier, in with me. It was a beautiful evening, and the drive all the more enjoyable, because the worst part of the move was over.

We arrived in Cheltenham just as it was getting dark, and went straight to the home of Bill and Brenda Davis. From there, David was picked up by Bill Wills, and he and Snowy spent the night with them.

Wednesday, 22nd saw us rushing down Gloucester Road from one direction, as the removal vans came towards us, all arriving at 211 together. Again, we were blessed with a sunny day to unload, although the next day was very wet.

Our Victorian house seemed like a palace; compared with the small house we had left in Watford, it seemed enormous, added to which, there were now two less people in the house. Paul had left home in 1975, and John had remained in "digs" in Chesham, close to his job.

Chapter Fourteen

We had a wonderful welcome service, with a packed church. Several friends from Watford came to support us, and we felt very much at home, from the word 'go'.

On Sunday, 2nd September 1979, Bob preached at St Mark's, our main church, with approximately 200 members, for the first time. In the morning, he preached on the 'Voyage of Life', in which he likened the Christian life to Sir Francis Chichester's epic, single-handed voyage round the world in the yacht 'Gypsy Moth IV'. He talked of the single-mindedness in reaching each 'staging post', the first one being Sydney, Australia, hopefully in 100 days, and the second, Plymouth, and home.

Bob said:
There are people who go through life, and haven't clue where they're going. They have little direction to their life, and consequently feel that life holds nothing for them. They are, as the title of a pop record suggests "Here, there and everywhere", but find themselves getting nowhere. The Christian life has a beginning, and it has a destination. The Christian, too, must know where he is going so that nothing will distract him from reaching his goal, or haven of rest.

I think sometimes, that we too can become earthbound, and feel that all that's worthwhile must be in terms of material prosperity or economic security. Real life in Christ has no end, and not even death can alter anything. Life in Christ, or Eternal Life, is of such quality, that it lasts for ever.

He went on to say,
Whenever a person sets out on the Christian Life, he is asked by Jesus, to count the cost - to consider seriously, the implications of being a disciple - life might not be all plain-sailing, 'Indeed, there may be ordeals and trials to which the Christian will be subjected. Becoming a Christian by no means excludes us from the possibility of suffering, or makes us immune from the trials and disasters of life. If this was true, religion would be the best kind of insurance policy anyone could wish for. No! We are asked to

prepare ourselves to meet anything that comes our way, in the right way.

Not even Jesus was excluded from the human lot, in fact, He faced suffering more acutely - mental, physical and spiritual agony. When faced with the reality of the Cross, and the horror of crucifixion, Jesus, in the Garden of Gethsemane, sought deliverance, but concluded His prayer with these words: "Not my will, but thine be done!" When St Paul sought release from some particular affliction, he pleaded desperately, "Three times I besought the Lord about this, that it should leave me, but He said to me, My grace is sufficient for you". As Christians, we must face the possibility, indeed the reality, even disaster, knowing, that whatever happens, we cannot drift beyond His love and care. ...... We cannot hope to complete the voyage of life, with all its trials and ordeals, as well as the blessings of smooth travel, alone. It is not our own individual skill and ability which will win the day, but on how far we are prepared to go into partnership. The words of another pop song are relevant, "Go it alone, go it alone; there is no need to go it alone"- yet, how often we try to do just that. No wonder we find the going tough. The Christian life is really partnership with Christ and our fellow Christians. In his letters St Paul constantly refers to the Church as the body of Christ, and each one of us as organs and limbs in that body, each doing an important job, thus maintaining the fitness and strength of the whole. So whoever we are, or however small our talents and gifts might be, they are necessary, and just as important as the gifts and talents of the outstanding Christian.

Partnership - Fellowship. Each of these words, has in them, a maritime term 'ship'. I distinctly remember an old Local Preacher in the North East of England tell, in his own language, what the word "Fellowship" meant. "Fellows in a ship", in other words, we're all in the same boat together, and therefore, we must seek to help each other. But the fellowship is further enriched by the Living Christ as the 'Skipper' at the helm. So may we, together, and with Christ, continue, the Voyage of Life.

Fine words for the beginning of a new stage of Ministry in Cheltenham and perhaps even more meaningful, because within the last few weeks we had seen a disastrous Fastnet boat race, with many killed in shipwrecks in atrocious weather, and within the last week, the death of Lord Mountbatten, whose boat was blown up off the coast of Ireland.

In the evening he preached on "Put out into the Deep", the three points of his sermon being 'The Deep of Failure', 'The Deep of Obedience' and 'The Deep of Unity'.

After his opening words about his experience (or lack of it!) in fishing, and the disappointment of catching nothing, time after time - which may explain his lack of interest later in life - he continued:-

'Master!' said Peter, 'we toiled all night and caught nothing', The sad confession of a man who knew the sea.

That sad confession is descriptive of English Church life in general today. There has been much denominational toil. Some Christians have even got so far as to say that their particular brand of Christianity is nearest to the mind of Jesus. Money and energy is ploughed into all kinds of schemes. The Organisation of the Church grinds on, but with little to show for the work. Plenty of toil, but no catch. In the Methodist Church alone the past year has seen a decrease in membership of 10,959. The number of men offering as candidates for the Ministry has also dropped considerably, as it has in other Churches.

What do Peter's words say to us? Just this. It is easy to be discouraged. In many places the Church does not give the appearance of being militant, but rather defeatist in attitude, and, like the fishermen in our lesson, in a deep of failure. So many Church members may be on the verge of giving up, and laying down their nets. Maybe some of us are conscious that we've been toiling, toiling, toiling - for years, and taken nothing, and there's a spirit of resignation abroad. We say 'What's the use?' No matter how discouraged the Church may be, God would have us continue in our work, recognising our failures. 'Lord, we have toiled all night and taken nothing'.

From the experience of failure as a fisherman, and in the presence of Jesus, Peter cries 'Depart from me, for I am a sinful man O Lord'. I don't think Peter really meant that. Oh yes, he knew he was a sinner - he knew he'd failed, but oh boy, he knew too, that Jesus was the only one who could meet his deepest need. In one of the Beatles' great hits, the song 'Yesterday' contains these words which certainly ring all kinds of bells, in the experience of us all, at times. The words are these:- 'I'm not half the man I used to be, there's a shadow hanging over me'. If we're honest, we'll cry with Peter, but we don't really want it to happen, 'Depart from me, for I am a sinful man, O Lord'.

Remember the American father, who was trying to encourage his dejected son by saying; 'Don't ever give up!' The boy replied, 'But I can't solve my problems'. The father replies, 'People who are remembered never gave up. Think of George Washington, Abraham Lincoln, Dr Martin Luther King Junior, they didn't give up. And look at Isador McPringle. The boy said 'But who is Isador McPringle?' 'See' said the father, 'you've never heard of him. He gave up!'

However much we've failed in the past, the Grace, Mercy and Forgiveness of God is available to every one of us, here and now.

The Deep of Obedience 'Master, we toiled all night, and took nothing! But, at your word, I will let down the nets. And when they had done this, they enclosed a great shoal of fish'.

Peter could, no doubt, have argued with Jesus, about the pros and cons of fishing. Peter was a fisherman, Jesus a carpenter. Peter could easily have reasoned with Jesus: 'Well, Master, you know all about wood and nails, but I've been at this business of fishing from my earliest years, and I know that this is not the time to fish. We go out at night, for that is the time to take fish. The glare of the morning sun on the silvery water causes the fish to hide. Jesus, this is not the time to fish!' But though Christ was a carpenter, and Peter a fisherman, yet Peter responded to the command of his Lord, and let down his net. Experience and reason would have said 'No', but Jesus said 'Yes let down your nets' and Peter obeyed. Obedience is easier said than done. It is easier to follow our own whims and fancies, to follow what we think best for the Kingdom of God, but, in doing so, we may not be obedient to Christ. The Church should always be asking, 'What would Christ have us do, here and now, in this situation, in that situation?' It is so easy for the Church to become insular, inward looking, and surely, the Church is only the Church when she looks beyond herself.

Finally, _The Deep of Unity._ 'Master, we toiled all night and took nothing! But, at your word, I will let down the nets. And when they had done this, they enclosed a great shoal of fish; and as their nets were breaking, they beckoned to their partners in the other boat, to come and help them. And they came, and filled both the boats.'

'They beckoned to their partners in the other boat'. What a delightful touch this is: They beckoned to their partners. They called for the support of the other fishermen, to assist them in their task. I'm quite sure, that church life would be far more successful and rewarding, if we could learn the secret of sharing. It is easy for each department to be concerned about its own life and work, and that we have little interest or concern for what is being attempted in the other departments. The ideal Church, is one in which there is a constant beckoning unto the partners, where all work together, and where all have a common desire to reach out after others.

The 20th century will probably be regarded in the future, as one of the most exciting periods in Church History. Already it has seen the formation of Councils of Churches on a local level, on a national level, and now, on an international level. The World Council of Churches stands as a witness to the real unity, which exists between churches of differing traditions......

There's a story told of a little bird, that went to see a wise old owl, to ask a question. 'What is the weight of a snowflake?' 'A snowflake doesn't weigh anything', replied the owl. But the little bird wasn't satisfied, and so it began to count, as snowflakes began to settle on a tree. Ten million - ten million and one, as the branch began to bend under the weight. Ten million and two as the branch of the tree finally broke!

Let me end, with a quotation from Mother Teresa of Calcutta. She said, 'Christian Unity is very important, because Christians stand for light for the world. If we are Christians, we must be Christ-like.' Ghandi once said that 'if Christians lived their life to the full, there would be no Hindus left in India.' That is what people expect of us, that we live our Christian life to the full. The first Christians died for Jesus, and were recognised because they loved one another, and the world has never needed more love than today.

And so began our Ministry in Cheltenham. I say our Ministry, because, for the first time, I became an active member of the 'team'. Before our move to Cheltenham, I had always tried to help and support Bob to the best of my ability, but always in the background; now, as a Local Preacher 'On Trial', I found myself in the 'front line'. It was perhaps, timely, that my role in Bob's Ministry should change then. The girls were growing up, Rachael was 7 and a half, and Sarah 4 and a half, when we moved, and both were at school, full time, and so, my 'permanent' excuse for not getting involved was, slowly, drifting out of the window. It was a case of either finding my niche as a housewife and mother within the Methodist Ministry, complementing Bob's work, (and I virtually had a free choice as to what I did), or looking outside for a job that would occupy much of my time.

Chapter Fifteen

The first months in a new Circuit are a time to take stock of what is happening; to get to know and understand people, and also to see any problems, that too often, you miss as the years go on, because you become too close to the situation. Our first quarter in Cheltenham was no exception. Methodists still tend to think in 'quarters' because the whole system is geared to that. The Preaching Plan is usually a 3-monthly one, many of the committees meet 4 times a year, and, until recently, the Ministers' stipends were paid quarterly on Sept. 1st, December 1st, March 1st and June 1st, quite a test, at first, for your budgeting abilities! These days, you can choose to have your stipend paid monthly if you wish.

We had pastoral charge of 4 churches, with 200 or so members at St Mark's, less than 50 at St Nicolas, and about a dozen each at Shipton Oliffe and Andoversford. St Mark's was next door to the Manse, and at that stage of our Ministry, we found it most helpful, although we were always careful not to allow the Manse to become an extension of the Church. The girls were able to take themselves off to Girls Brigade, Junior Church, Choir Practice, and anything else they wished to go to, on their own, without our having to sort out transport problems. Mum, too, was able to be independent, and 'do her own thing'.

Bob was always very good at learning people's names, and before we had been in the Circuit many weeks was, as usual, well-versed with who people were, their names, their jobs, their families etc. It always took me a lot longer. For what seemed like years, I would be smiling at people as Bob and I passed them in the street, and at the same time, muttering out of the corner of my mouth, "Who's that?"

Our predecessor, Rev John Appleby, had formed a group for the housebound, which met on the first Friday afternoon of every month (called Friday Club!), with the fit and able-bodied transporting the members to and from the Church, where entertainment, a 'shop' and tea (sandwiches, cakes etc.) were laid on. For those unable to get into a car, a 'wheelchair bus' was laid on. This was borrowed from the Ambulance Station, and the driver had to satisfy those responsible that he could handle the vehicle satisfactorily. Within days of starting work, Bob realised that he was expected to drive it, because John always had, but there was no time to sort it out, and so the 'deputy' had to do it that September. Bob started his duties in October and although he eventually found it too time-consuming and organised another driver, he always went in to see everyone and usually had tea with them.

Another 'rude awakening' was at the end of his first service at St Mark's, when Olive Etchells, editor of the Church Magazine 'The Messenger', approached Bob and asked for his 'Minister's Letter'. He asked when the deadline was, and she said "Now!" followed by "I did warn you!" In the chaos of moving, Bob had forgotten all about it. That afternoon was spent in the study!! The other memorable highlight of those early months in Cheltenham was the carol service. Having spent 7 years in Watford, where there was no choir during our time, the joy of hearing the choir as we celebrated our Saviour's birth was wonderful.

But our other churches were a joy, too. St Nicolas had problems caused by sharing their premises, but we always had a wonderful welcome. It also enabled us to renew our friendship with Geoff and Betty Dorey, who had been members at my home church at South Harrow, and had visited us several times in St Austell. They moved from Harrow to Cheltenham with Geoff's job in 1972, just as we were leaving St Austell for Watford! By sheer coincidence, they became members of ours on our move to Cheltenham, and the friendship deepened and blossomed over the years.

Shipton Oliffe Methodist Church had the distinction of being the only brick-built building in the whole of a delightful little Cotswold village. Almost a hundred years old at the time of our arrival, you could just picture a land owner giving the early Methodists in the village, a strip of land on the edge of a field, and them building their church with the best materials that they could afford - red brick. The result was a unique church, long and narrow, with a centre pulpit, a hand-pumped organ (even in 1979), a pot-bellied stove, with a pipe that went out through the roof, and wooden benches to sit on. The tiny vestry was also used if refreshments were to be served after a service.

Bob was always very particular about his appearance, and especially if he was either preaching or on official business. If he was taking a service of Holy Communion, his always well-polished shoes, were given an extra good shine, because it is when people kneel at the communion rail, that their eyes focus on the Minister's feet; and immediately before leaving home, a good 5 minutes or more was spent with a nail brush, scrubbing his hands, because no-one wants to receive the elements at the Lord's Supper from a pair of rather dubious hands. In the vestry, before a 'normal' service, Bob's last action was to look in a mirror and comb his hair if necessary. At Shipton Oliffe, they had no mirror; Bob, as much in fun as in anything else, protested loudly. Next time he preached, a handbag mirror had appeared, but that still wasn't good enough - he couldn't see all of his head in it! Then a 'porthole' style mirror came, but that still didn't work, and so, for the extent of our stay in the Cheltenham Circuit, he and the Steward, Doss Enstone, teased each other before the service, about the mirror, and Bob's hair!

Andoversford, was only a mile away from Shipton, but very different. The Church itself was in the middle of a row of cottages. In fact, originally, it had been a tiny cottage, but over a hundred years ago, the whole of the inside had been taken out, to form one large room (apart from a tiny, tiny entrance hall, with a curtain across it, to shut it off from the Church itself). Inside were 36 wooden chairs, a pulpit in the left hand corner as you faced it, a slightly raised communion area, and a tiny communion rail that had just enough room for four people. There was an arched window above the door, and another one opposite, behind and above the Communion Table, and at certain times of the year, when the sun hit the window by the door at just the right angle, during the evening service, it very nearly sent the entire congregation to sleep. Many times, when I've been with Bob to an evening service, I have struggled to keep awake! I don't know what the neighbours thought of our singing, I suppose they accepted it as a matter of course; they knew it was a Church when they moved in, just as we accepted an occasional flush of the toilet during a service!

Both our village churches (not chapels!!) were a breath of fresh air and a total change from St Mark's and St Nicolas; we loved going out to them, even the seven mile drive to them was relaxing. As often as we possibly could, we went to our three smaller churches together. I felt, very strongly, that they had as much right to me, as their Minister's wife, as St Mark's did, and we felt much loved, especially in the small communities in the country. The girls loved going out there, too, and we took them whenever there was a special service. At Shipton, there was a ford, just a hundred yards or so from the church; it also had a tiny bridge. The water was always very clear and shallow, and they loved playing "Pooh Sticks", dropping sticks in the water, one each, and seeing which one floated out from the other side of the bridge first. It's a game Winnie-the-Pooh played, hence its name. Gradually other children from the town churches came out with their families, and more and more were seen hanging over the bridge!

Before we had chance to collect ourselves, it was harvest time, and all four Harvest Thanksgivings were different - Bob preferred 'Thanksgiving' to 'Festival'. St Nicolas celebrated, as far as I remember, on the same day as the Church of England, but not a United Service, much to Bob's disappointment. St Mark's traditionally supported the Methodist Relief and Development Fund, and had a token display of produce, which seemed very strange to us, at first. Their Harvest Supper was on the Saturday night, and normally entailed a meal, followed by entertainment - usually home grown, and with lots of laughs. On the Monday morning, the produce was distributed, although it got harder and harder, as the years went on, to find people who wanted it, everywhere was inundated with the results of Harvests at schools, at women's groups, both church and secular, at pubs, as well as the many churches in Cheltenham.

Andoversford always looked very pretty for the Harvest, and the local members made sure that the right local people received their gifts. They just had one service at 6.00 p.m.

Shipton would also be beautifully decorated, but the outstanding sight, as you walked through the doors, was the stove. Every inch of it was covered with corn, fruit and vegetables, you really felt it was harvest time, and the time to give thanks that 'All is safely gathered in".

Although we were never aware of any culture shock after leaving Watford, I suppose our happiness at being in such a beautiful place was the shock, or all we were going to experience of it. We settled immediately, and never looked back, or should I say Mum, Rachael, Sarah and I never looked back, for Bob always had the policy that when you finally shut the front door of the Manse you are leaving, you forget it all, and concentrate on your new Circuit.

At this point, you may be wondering "Where's David?" Well, David left school in Watford, after his G.C.E's (General Certificate of Education), in the summer of 1979. He had hoped to be enlisted in the R.A.F. but was turned down because of his tendency to eczema on his hands, a problem that he'd had since he was a little boy, but that was improving all the time. Within two weeks of our arrival in Cheltenham, he had found himself a job as a trainee chef in a hotel in Chipping Campden - The Noel Arms - about 22 miles away. He lived in, and came home for his two days off each week, but as he made friends in the area, the visits home became less and less frequent, and we breathed a huge sigh of relief, in the knowledge that he was settled and making a new life for himself.

And so, our first year in Cheltenham flew by, and as we entered the summer period, all the signs appeared, advertising soft fruit for sale at almost every farm we went past. The whole of the Cheltenham/ Evesham area is renowned for its soft fruit, something we were quite naive about until we got there!

One day, we had our friends, Kath and Keith Bass, from Watford, staying with us, and David had been home too, so we decided to drop him back at work, and to go on to pick some strawberries somewhere. Before very long, we saw a huge sign saying 'Pick Your Own Strawberries ahead'. We drove along for a mile or so, and suddenly, I saw a sign. Bob seemed to be oblivious to it, so from my back seat, I tapped him on the shoulder, and yelled in his ear "P.Y.O., turn left". Instead of turning, he proceeded to argue the toss, saying "What on earth is P.Y.O.?" We just about made the left hand turn, but Kath, Keith and I were curled up with laughter by then, and Bob still couldn't work out what P.Y.O was!

But the one thing that is synonymous with Cheltenham is the Gold Cup. For the uninitiated, the Gold Cup is the main horse race (steeplechase) in an event that lasts three days. For many people in Ireland it is the highlight of their year, and many save from one Gold Cup to the next in order to get there. The town doubles in size that week, and it's almost impossible to get into shops in the mornings. The afternoons are O.K. - everyone's at the races! At the end of the day, traffic leaving the town is horrendous. Church meetings are arranged to avoid Gold Cup Week if possible. It is usually held around about 17th March, (that is St Patrick's Day, but I think that's a coincidence) and all sorts of weather is possible during that week, even snow. The weather can be glorious, and then change on Gold Cup day, and it has been known to change just for an hour or so at race time!

So, also in that first year, we had our initiation into Gold Cup Week. One of our older members, a lovely lady, Cicely Powis, from Shipton, made the comment, when talking about 'locals' opening up for Bed and Breakfast, just for that week, said, "Oh yes, it's all feet to the pole in some houses!" Bob could sometimes totally miss the point, much to the family's amusement, and he got teased on this occasion, when I had to explain that it was an old saying from the days of 'Bell' or round tents. You got more people in if they all put their feet to the centre pole!

The family together before we left Watford in 1979. Back row, from the left: John, David, Paul. Front Row, from the left: Sarah, Bob, Joy, Rachael.

One of many Church Stewards Christmas Parties, in the Manse in Cheltenham

Worship in the little Methodist Church at Shipton Oliffe, in the Cheltenham Circuit.

Cheltenham 1981. Local Preachers Recognition Service for Joy and also Richard Courtney. From the left: Bob, Ian Lunn - Chair of Bristol District – John Newton – President of the Methodist Conference – Joy, Richard, David Ratcliffe – Superintendent of the Cheltenham Circuit.

A church outing from St Mark's, Cheltenham. At Hannam Mount, Bristol, where John Wesley preached in the open air. Friends, Kath and Keith Bass, from North Watford, joined us for that occasion.

St Mark's, Cheltenham. Easter breakfast.

Bob with the St Mark's Easter banner, preparing for the 8am Service, which began outside.

Bob on Christmas morning at St Mark's. He always complained that he never had a teddy, so the church gave him one!

Chapter Sixteen

1981 was the Centenary of the beginning of St Mark's. A group of people had come from another Methodist Church in the town, Bethesda and held services under a gas lamp by the railway station, 100 yards up the road from where St Mark's stands now. The fellowship grew, and eventually, the Church was built, and opened in 1911. As many of the older members had memories going back that far, it was felt that the Centenary of the founding of the Fellowship should be celebrated, rather than the Centenary of the building, when those who would be around to celebrate it would not have such wonderful memories. The planning would take some time, and so it began in 1980.

The planning committee suggested, and the Church agreed, that the celebrations should be spread over the whole year, with the major weekend being the first weekend of November - the time which was usually observed as Church Anniversary Weekend. Every month, a past Minister or Local Preacher was invited to preach, and many happy reunions took place.

The weekend of 24th May, 1981, Wesley Day, which just happened to fall on a Sunday that year, was planned with a former minister, Rev Maurice Jelbert, as the preacher, morning and evening. Sadly, early in the year Maurice died, very suddenly, and the planning committee were at a loss about what to do. Bob had asked the Speaker of the House of Commons, George Thomas, to preach in Watford, but he was unable to, so he thought it was worth another try. Everyone was delighted when he replied, accepting the invitation for the morning, but not the evening, because he had to be in London for the unveiling of the Aldersgate Memorial to John Wesley, by the Prime Minister, Margaret Thatcher.

And so, with great anticipation, we began 1981, but before the first week was out, we had a 'phone call from Paul, telling us that he and his fiancée, Therese, had got fed up with waiting to get married, and had found a flat, and planned to marry on 27th January (1981) in Halifax. We went almost straight out to get clothes sorted out for Rachael and Sarah for the wedding. Bob's suit was fine, and I just needed a coat. Fortunately, it was the right time for the New Year Sales.

In the six years Paul had been in Halifax, after working in a supermarket briefly, he had trained and qualified as a nurse; he enjoyed the work so much that he decided that he would like to train as a doctor, but, before he could do that, he had to get 3 'A' Level examinations in the Sciences. For two years, he worked part-time nights at one hospital, and did a full-time college course. Birmingham University Medical School accepted him on condition that he obtained 3 'A' grades. He worked extremely hard, and achieved 'A' grades in all 3 subjects.

It was the January before he was due to take his 'A' Levels that they decided to get married. We were pleased, because it meant that they would have six months to adjust to married life, before they had to move away from the area to start at Medical School. It was just the 3 weeks notice that took our breath away!

Both David and John were able to get time off work for the Tuesday wedding, and we had a lovely day. We had not been able to meet Therese before the wedding, but as we got to know her, we grew to love her very, very much, and now, it just feels as if she's always been part of our family. Bob often teased her, though, and told her that he got a 'Pig in a Poke' when he got her, in other words he bought her before he'd seen her!!!

Therese is a devout Roman Catholic, and they were married in the small Roman Catholic Church at Mixenden, Halifax. Bob was so very thrilled when he was asked to deliver the homily at the wedding.

After the excitement of that January, life settled down again, and I prepared myself for the last of my four written Local Preachers' exams, to be taken in the middle of April. All went well; I passed, and breathed a sigh of relief. The next step was an Oral Examination in front of the Local Preachers of the Circuit, due to take place on Wednesday, 20th May, 1981.

At the beginning of May, my Mother took a break, and went to visit my brother in Scotland. She went for two weeks, but during her second week, Sarah began to feel unwell. She was at the Doctor's almost every day, with different symptoms, and gradually getting worse. I was trying to get Rachael sorted out for her first experience of camp with the Girls Brigade, and so life was very fraught. Eventually, late on the Friday afternoon, after yet another visit to the Doctor, a diagnosis looked possible, but would only be confirmed after hospital tests. She was admitted to the Children's Hospital at Battledown, Cheltenham, after we had waved Rachael off to camp.

Once she had been admitted to hospital, Sarah was kept in isolation for the whole week that she was there. She was diagnosed with Stevens - Johnson syndrome [with the advances of science, it is now thought that it was more likely to have been Kawasaki Disease], probably brought on by a virus. It initially attacked all her saliva glands, and then worked its way through her body, affecting her hair last - about 1-2 months later.

She was kept in hospital, mainly to be nursed, as no treatment was possible, we just had to let the virus work its way through her system. After a week, the doctors decided that she was well enough to go home. During that week she had been inundated with visitors, all bringing gifts - her soft toy collection grew considerably, but poor Rachael really felt left out; she said "I would like to be ill, not really ill, but just enough to get presents."

The Wednesday of the week she was in hospital was - you've guessed it - 20th May. I had done all my preparation, and wanted to have a go at the exam, after all, if I failed, I would at least know what I was in for next time. Bob was in total agreement, and we both knew, that if Sarah wasn't well enough to be left then I would pull out. One of our colleagues was worried in case I got preferential treatment - a sympathy vote and so we requested that nothing at all should be said about it, until the end of the meeting. All went well, and I breathed a huge sigh of relief when told I had passed. That left the final hurdle, a Trial Service in front of a Minister and a Local Preacher. Mine took place on the evening of 12th July, 1981, at Winchcombe Methodist Church, with a good report, and the recommendation that I be 'officially recognised' as a Local Preacher.

Sarah came out of hospital, at 9.00 a.m. on 23rd May, the day before George Thomas' visit. She had lost a lot of weight, and was skin and bone, but determined to go to Church for the "big do". She was only 6 years old, but knew exactly what was going on.

On the Sunday morning, George arrived at 9.00 a.m. at the Manse, and we had a wonderful time of fellowship with him, until it was time to go across to the Church. He really put us at our ease. He played with the children, joked with the adults, and in that short time, made us feel as if we had known him all our lives.

The service was an amazing experience, and enjoyed by adults and children alike. An audio tape was made, and even 14 years later, people told me that they still listened to it regularly, and still appreciated the message. The one thing George forgot to do, was to give everyone his catchphrase, 'Order, Order', during the service, although he did say it in the hall, over coffee.

As a direct result of George's visit, we were invited to tea with him at 'Speaker's House', inside the Houses of Parliament, in London. The arrangements were made, and we were told that, on Monday, 13th July, we were to arrive at the House of Commons via St Stephen's entrance, and ask to be directed to the Lobby. At 2.15 p.m. we could pick up our tickets from the Police Officer in attendance. "After the Speaker's procession, which is just before 2.30 p.m., you should make your way to the Distinguished Strangers' Gallery (the Police Officer will direct you).
At 4.50 p.m., would you leave the Gallery and ask the Door Keeper if he will have you taken to the Speaker's Office, where one of us will take you to the residence". These were the instructions sent from the Speaker's Office, on 19th June 1981.

Our holiday, that year, was extremely early, at the beginning of June. It was not of our choosing, but the only dates that were available for the flat at Grange-over-Sands, on the edge of the Lake District, which we were able to rent quite cheaply from the Invalid Ministers' Rest Fund, and available only to Methodist Ministers. In the end, it was a blessing because, only two weeks after she came out of hospital, we were able to take Sarah away for a break. During that holiday we spent a day with Paul and Therese in their flat, the first time we had seen them since the wedding. We had a lovely day, calling at Howarth, home of the Bronte sisters, on the way. As a family, we have never forgotten that occasion, because never having had 5 extra (Joy, Bob, Rachael, Sarah and Grandma) for a meal, they had over-estimated how much we would eat, and cooked two large chickens. Bob teased them for years about it, not only on the amount of chicken he ate, but also how many days, weeks, years(!) they were eating the leftovers!

The early holiday also followed, very closely, Bob's sponsored walk. This was the first of several that he did in Cheltenham for various 'good causes', and took place two days after George Thomas' visit.

Early in the morning, on 26th May, 1981, Bob set off on a 25 mile walk around part of the Cheltenham Circuit. He left St Mark's, went via

Bethesda, St Matthew's and Whaddon Methodist Churches, to Battledown, over Harp Hill, Ham, Ham Hill, Whittington and on to Shipton Oliffe and a lunch stop. After a break, it was down to Andoversford, Dowdeswell, Charlton Kings, Leckhampton, and back to St Mark's. The money he raised went to the 'Cheltenham and District Swimming and Athletic Club for the Disabled'. He had company all the way, but most walked a few miles, and then swapped with someone else. John Noton, a member at St Mark's, started off with Bob, saying he would just walk to the edge of the town, but in the end, he did the whole 25 miles, an amazing feat, considering he had retired several years before.

Sarah had to go back to the hospital that day, so I was not able to walk with Bob, but after lunch, one of the support team came back for me, and I joined him just before he reached the left turn to Charlton Kings, from the A40. We arrived home at about 5.00 p.m., and I seem to remember our going out to an evening meeting afterwards!

1981 was quite an eventful year. In the spring, Prince Charles had announced his engagement to Lady Diana Spencer, and a property had been bought in Gloucestershire, which was to be their home. In the March (Friday, 27th), they both came to visit the Headquarters of the Gloucestershire Police, flying in by helicopter, and landing about a mile from the Manse, on the playing field of Dean Close School.

Bob continued to pretend that he was an anti-royalist as he did in St Austell, and this occasion was just the same. He made a big 'thing' about taking me to see them, and what a big favour he was doing me, but he was the disappointed one, when the car went past us so fast that he was unable to get a photograph. He complained all the way home, and, in the end, I suggested that they were only here for an hour, why didn't he go back for another try? And so, after a cup of coffee, we went off down the road. This time, Bob again picked what he felt was the best spot, but with the advantage of the experience an hour before. When they arrived back, one or two people jumped the Police cordon, and ran towards the helicopter, that was enough for Bob. He was gone, but no-one was more surprised than he, when he found himself, face to face with the Royal couple, and only a couple of feet away! He just took a photo! When it was developed no-one at first believed that he'd taken it, and certainly not face to face. He must have used a telephoto lens, or something. However, once his achievement was acknowledged, a copy appeared on the front of the Church Magazine. It was printed in the June, 1981 copy of 'Cotswold Life' with the comment, "The Reverend

Robert Wilson of Cheltenham, considered himself extremely fortunate to have been able to snap H.R.H. The Prince of Wales and Lady Diana Spencer on their recent 'flying' visit to the town. The couple are seen here about to board a helicopter as the visit came to an end", and Bob gave away numerous copies. But he still maintained that he wasn't a Royalist!

On the evening of 12th July, after my Trial Service, we left home for Watford, and from there went to the flat of a friend, Margaret Adamson, in Hatfield, where we stayed the night. By doing this, we had no need to rush off the next morning. After a leisurely breakfast, we made our way to London, and Westminster, arriving in time, we thought, to spend some time in the Abbey, but we were unable to go very far in, so we went into the gift shop, buying the girls odds and ends to keep them amused while we were sitting in the Gallery of the House of Commons, and I also bought Bob a polished wooden cross, with a thin, gold cross inlaid on the front, and when hung on a leather thong, he wore it on all official occasions, whether preaching or visiting. If he wore his clerical collar, he wore his cross. When our souvenirs of the occasion were all paid for, we went for a walk around the outside of Parliament, before finally making our way inside.

Having been given our tickets, we were told that we could take nothing in with us, not even the children's books, so we handed it all over, and waited for the Speaker's Procession. What a thrill to see George in all his regalia, right in front of us! Once the procession had passed through we were taken up to our seats - right in the front row of the Gallery! The Speaker's Chair was opposite us, and although the adults (Joy, Bob and Grandma) found it fascinating, to the girls it was deadly boring; after all, Rachael was only nine and Sarah only six. George waved to them, discreetly, from his chair, but in the end, they fell asleep. At about 4.30 p.m. George left his chair, and the Deputy Speaker took over. Bob told the girls that he'd gone to put the kettle on! Well before 4.50 p.m. an attendant came up to us, and asked us to follow him, and we were led through what appeared to be the library, and around some narrow corridors, up in a lift, and into the entrance hall of the private flat, at the top of Speaker's House. George made us very much at home, and encouraged the girls to climb on to the window seat to look at the river (Thames) below. Tea was brought in and we chatted together, like old friends. After a while, one of George's staff came in to tell him that Lord Soames had arrived to see him, so there were some rather hurried photographs taken, before George disappeared, leaving instructions that we were to be shown the 'State' Rooms in 'Speaker's House'. The dining room was being prepared for a banquet. Mr Speaker was entertaining the Prime Minister, Margaret Thatcher, and her Cabinet, that evening. We were also shown the portraits and coats of arms of all the Speakers of the House, including George's. We even had a close look at the Speaker's wig, which amused the girls. The occasion was all the more exciting, because it was only two weeks before the Royal wedding, and it had just been announced that Prince Charles had asked George to read the lesson - 1 Corinthians 13 - at the wedding. He was delighted. All in all, an occasion to remember, and we all treasured it, but Bob especially so.

After the summer holidays, life began to settle into some form of normality – at least, for a few weeks! But before very long, the preparations for the 'big weekend' really began to get underway. As 1st November was the Sunday, our celebrations began on Saturday, 31st October. Bob was expected to be around to receive gifts of money between 10.00 a.m. and noon, and again between 2.00p.m. and 4.00 p.m. This was an annual occurrence, and if there was a good stream of people, he really enjoyed it, but if not many people turned up (they put their gifts in the Offering next day), it was deadly dull. While this was going on, there was an exhibition of old photographs and slides of the Church and members in one of the side rooms. The Centenary Dinner was taken in two sittings, and the delicious hot meal, was a real credit to the hard work put in by the catering team.

Being at the Centenary Dinner, Bob was expected to deliver a brief speech, and judging by his notes, it was fairly brief, although, I'm sure that there were lots of 'ad libs' of which I have no record. He said:
It was one Sunday morning last year, when I was preaching at an 11.00 a.m. service, either at St Matthew's or Bethesda, and I did my usual custom, of being at the door of St Mark's, greeting our people, as they came in. I heard the first hymn announced by the preacher, and was making my way to the car, when I was stopped by some strangers, on the other side of the road. A man and his wife and two children. They were obviously visitors to Cheltenham, but the husband asked me this question: 'Did I know where they could find a lively Methodist Church?' - whatever he meant by lively! Now I've no idea, whether or not, they came to the service at St Mark's, but the husband's comment, reminded me of a story I heard a long time ago.

It was about an Evangelist, who conducted a 10 day mission at a Church in San Francisco. Each evening the Evangelist noticed Chinese men, sitting in the front seats. They were the best prayers, the best singers, and the best workers in the meetings. At the end of the 10 days, the Campaign was over, and the Evangelist left. Six months later, that same Evangelist, went back to conduct a follow-up campaign, and he noticed that the six Chinese men were missing, and they never once appeared during the follow-up meetings. The Evangelist asked the Minister of the Church where the Chinese men were, for they were there when he conducted the initial campaign. Said the Minister: 'O dear, we had to turn them out (in other words excommunicate them). Yes, we had to turn them out of the Church; they were full of bed bugs', to which the Evangelist replied: 'When you turned those Chinese men and bed bugs out, you turned out the only live things in this Church!'

Now you may wonder what on earth a story about Chinese men and bed bugs has to do with our Centenary Dinner, and the return of the Rev Alan Merritt. I'm beginning to wonder myself. It's 17 years since Alan Merritt (a much younger man in those days) left St Mark's. No doubt he's been back since then, and I know, for sure, that he receives the Messenger (Church Magazine) each month. I hope the present state of our Church life indicates that the Church is alive, and healthy, and seeking to make its mark and contribution to the life of the wider community.

We haven't got any Chinese men in our congregation yet, but I know there are a great number of caring people, and people with vision and with a grasp of what the Kingdom of God is all about. One thing is certain, when the People Called Methodists, in the year 2081 celebrate the Bi-Centenary of the founding of the Society, none of us will be present (at least, not in the flesh), but just as the foundation of the work was laid by the faith, the vision, and the inspiration of that small group who met under the lamp, where we will meet tomorrow morning, so may we build here a community of love and trust, of understanding, and above all, united in our endeavour, and by the Grace of God, prepare for the future, which stretches out in front of us.

There followed comments by other Church officials, and also the guest preacher for the Sunday, Alan Merritt, but by about 8.45 p.m. the meal was finished, the tables moved out of the way, and all was ready for the Church Family Concert - all 'home-grown' talent, and very enjoyable.

After a short break, for some sleep we were back at the Church, in time for an 8.00 a.m. Service of Holy Communion! Bob both presided and preached, and the real stalwarts were all there. Bob's text was "Where there is no vision, the people perish" (Proverbs 29:18), and quoting from George Thomas' sermon on Wesley Day, said

We are all the Children of Giants. All Saints Day is an appropriate occasion for us, this Centenary Year, to celebrate the founding of the Methodist community in this part of Cheltenham ..... we, here this morning, are surrounded by that unseen host - that great cloud of witnesses, to which is added the faithful men and women, who, through almost 2,000 years, demonstrated, and showed their allegiance to Jesus..... So, you see, we are all children of Giants, but the question must be asked: have we the same sort of vision, or the same kind of faith, that enables us to surmount obstacles, in the cause of Christ's Kingdom? Ours is a faith that embraces not only the present, but the past and the future - eternity itself. That's why the Church is indestructible, and that is why, whilst it's true, that what Jesus said about 'no man who puts his hand to the plough, and then looks back, is fit for the Kingdom of God', we are justified today in allowing ourselves to indulge in a little nostalgia, and to thank God for those few people - men and women, who gathered 100 years ago, under the lamp, and from their faith, and their vision, we inherit and enjoy, the fruit of their labours.

Where there is no vision, the people perish. Thank God, that from our forefathers we can gain fresh courage and inspiration - so that, not continually looking back, we go forward in the strength and power of God, to serve in His name, and to provide here, a place of worship, a place of fellowship, and a place of service, ministering to the needs of all.

After the communion, we assembled in the hall for breakfast, but by 9.40 a.m. we were lined up outside, ready to literally 'follow the band' - Girls Brigade and Boys Brigade - to the site of the first meeting - the lamp. It is now situated on a traffic island at the junction of Queen's Road and Gloucester Road, and quite a group of us, Bob included, managed to stand on the island, for the brief service. The rest stood on the nearby pavement. Bob again preached, this time praising

Edward Parker and Samuel Randle, who led mission workers from Bethesda, in starting Open Air Services under the Lamp, on Lansdown Railway Bridge ..... they exalted the name of Jesus, and proclaimed the Gospel of God's all-embracing love. We today, albeit in a different time, and a very different setting, still want to exalt the name of Jesus, and to offer the Grace of God to all. And why do we still want to offer such a gospel? Quite simply, that Society's search for wholeness of life, and the individual's quest for fulfilment, in a materialistic way, is futile. When St Augustine said: 'Our hearts are restless until they find rest in God', he was expressing a need which is still with us. That, even today, men and women (whether they realise it or not) need life, and need fulfilment, and that life and that fulfilment is found in Jesus Christ. Jesus said 'I have come, that they may have life, and have it more abundantly', and the Methodist people, through spiritual, social and political means, have sought to proclaim such a gospel that is concerned with the whole of man's life. In 1881, the first Methodist Society in this part of Cheltenham had its beginnings under the lamp. That same century, the Tolpuddle Martyrs, most of whom were Methodists, formed the first Agricultural Trade Union. To end with, something George Thomas, Speaker of the House of Commons, said when he preached at St Mark's Methodist Church, last May: 'We are all the Children of Giants, and our responsibility Today and in the Future, is to demonstrate the love of Christ, by caring for the needs of people of all ages.

After a brief prayer, we re-assembled, and again, following the band, marched back to the Church. We caused quite a stir. Gloucester Road is a very busy, main road, and we needed both Police permission to march, and a Police escort. We couldn't fail to be noticed.

Before we had time to turn around, it was 10.30 a.m. and time for Morning Worship. I'm sure Bob was very relieved that he had no more sermons to preach that day! Bob led both morning and evening worship, and Alan Merritt preached. It was a wonderful weekend, but the celebrations weren't over, yet!

On Tuesday, 3rd November, 1981, we were blessed by the visit of the President of the Methodist Conference, Rev Dr John A. Newton. He arrived during the afternoon, and once again, we assembled in the hall for food - this time, tea - sandwiches and cakes, and probably some salad too. Tea was from 5.30 p.m.-6.30 p.m., followed by half-an-hour for people to socialise. During this time, the Press arrived and took various photographs, and interviewed the President.

By sheer coincidence, I had, by now, completed my Local Preachers' studies, and was just awaiting my Recognition Service - a service which literally recognises that the training is complete, and from that moment on, the preacher is classed as Fully Accredited, and a preacher in their own right. Another Local Preacher, Richard Courtney, was at the same stage. I suppose that being married to a Minister does have some 'perks' and this was one of those occasions. Bob came up with the idea that Richard and I should be Recognised when the President of Conference was preaching, and also the Re-dedication of Local Preachers, together with a Local Preacher's Diploma to be presented to Janet Roe (now Rev Janet Roe, but then a Local Preacher 'On Trial', who did the Diploma first!), and also a certificate to Cicely Powis, who had just completed 60 years as organist at Shipton Oliffe Methodist Church. Not only was it a great occasion at St Mark's, it was also a great occasion for the Circuit, and one that I shall never forget. The evening was 'rounded off' with a time of fellowship and coffee in the Manse, with the President, the Chairman of the Bristol District - Rev Ian Lunn, and his wife, June, and our friends, Kath and Keith Bass, who were there, mainly to share with us as a family, at my Recognition Service.

As Christmas drew nearer, we began to get invitations to attend the Christmas celebrations with groups, both within the Church, and outside. These usually began at the beginning of December, and went on until we got to Christmas Day itself, by which time we were exhausted. This was especially so, if it worked out that we had the Carol Service followed by mince pies and coffee on one day, the Christmas Eve Holy Communion the next, and Christmas Morning Family Service the next. The girls still complain of the fact that instead of playing party games Bob, and I nearly always fell asleep for a short while after lunch, on Christmas Day.

Christmas 1981 was saddened by the news of the death of Bob's eldest sister Edna. She died very suddenly, on 17th December, and unbe-known to us she had cancer, and had been given two months to live. However, she died the day after the surgeons discovered it, and before hardly any of the family knew. Bob travelled up to Bedlington for her funeral on 22nd December, his birthday. He had to go alone, because of the cost of the train fare, and the time of year - I was tied up with all sorts of parties etc. with Rachael and Sarah. Had the weather been better (lots of snow all through December, and the worst winter we had in Cheltenham), and the car a reasonable proposition, I would have gone with him.

And so, 1981 came to a close. An exhausting year, not without its worry and sadness, but a memorable one, and one I wouldn't have missed for the world. We entered 1982, full of hope and anticipation, as we did every year, but there was the added excitement of another Pastoral Exchange to the U.S.A. that summer; this time, to the small town of Brunswick, Ohio, about 20 miles south-west of Cleveland.

Chapter Seventeen

December 1981 had been a very snowy month. The bad weather started at the beginning of the month, and after a brief lull, came back with a vengeance, nearer Christmas. By Christmas Day, the hard packed snow began to melt, and everyone breathed a sigh of relief. Therese and Paul came from Birmingham to spend part of Christmas with us, and we were delighted. Therese was due back on duty immediately after lunch on Christmas Day, so we had our Christmas Dinner on Christmas Eve; in fact, in the Wilson household, from mid-day onwards, Christmas Eve 1981 became Christmas Day. On Christmas morning we opened our gifts, went to church as a family, and then had a "cold meat and pickles" meal before driving Paul and Therese back to Birmingham. All the way there we saw remnants of the snow, and thanked God that, although it had been a white Christmas, it had not caused any of us any problems with regard to travelling. John had managed to get to us from Chesham, and David was able to call in as his duties at the hotel had allowed.

The New Year was fine, and the children started back to school, but before long, the snow hit us again, and everything ground to a halt for over a week. The schools closed; local radio warned people not to go out unless it was absolutely necessary; and of course, all church mid-week meetings were abandoned. One Sunday a few stragglers managed to get to the morning service, but we gave up on the evening one! In the Manse, we battened down the hatches, and enjoyed being together as a family. Access to the Church car park was by means of a long drive, which served the Manse as well; our garage was half way down, at right angles to the drive; normally the slope down from the main road was hardly noticeable (apart from the danger of toddlers' legs running away with them if they ran on ahead of the adults), but when covered with snow, it was a totally different thing!

The snow had blown in drifts down the drive, and in places reached Bob's thighs. He tried clearing a path for the car, but the right hand turn out of the garage, plus the slope, proved to be too much for the car and he had to accept, not with an easy conscience, that he was 'grounded'. I remember he went to help an elderly lady, who had very tentative Church links, and lived a good half hour's walk away, on a good day. She was panicking, and instead of contacting someone who lived nearby, he went himself; he was gone for hours, and by the time he returned home I had imagined that the hard and energy-draining struggle through the snow had brought on a heart attack, and he was lying dead in the street! Bob, as usual, could see no problem, "You knew it would take a while, of course I'm alright".

Our back door was piled up with snow, and the four steps down from it totally impassable. It was always quite draughty, but this time there was none - the snow sorted that one out! The local paper, the Gloucestershire Echo, had a competition to see who had the longest icicle, no-one bothered to send in a report on the ones hanging from the porch of the Church Hall - they must have been 3-4 feet long! I watched the depth of frost on the washing line grow, day by day; and Bob and I experienced freezing fog for the first time when walking to and from the school to collect the girls. The local park/gardens at Pittville were beautiful, with frost more than snow, turning it into a winter wonderland. I have experienced many bad winters, but 1981/82 is one I will remember for many many years - even the Queen was stranded near Bath when her Range Rover got stuck in snowdrifts, after a private visit to Princess Anne and her family at Gatcombe Park, near Stroud!

The snow eventually left us and our lives got back to normal. Years later, we found a tape that the girls had made while they were off school. Rachael describes the weather conditions and concludes with the comment, 'There are even policemen patrolling the streets!" I suppose she noticed them walking, rather than using cars.

And so, Easter came. In 1981 Bob had tried something new on Maundy Thursday (or at least new to St Mark's), and it had gone well, so it was decided to do it again in 1982. Instead of Holy Communion in the Church, we met in the hall, and everyone was seated on the outside of a square formed by tables. At various points were large candles - candles of defeat - these were alight, but put out during the service. Also on the tables were towels and bowls of water for us to wash each other's hands, and the Bread and Wine were in front of Bob's seat. We meditated together on the events in the Upper Room at the first Easter, and we sang Maundy Thursday hymns. This service became so popular that it became necessary to assemble in a side room so that the tables and seating could be arranged to accommodate everyone rather than a big upheaval when we went in. The last one that Bob took was so full that it was becoming a problem. How could we fit everyone in, and still retain the special atmosphere of the Last Supper? They must have resolved it, because at the time of writing, it was still the form of worship at St Mark's on Maundy Thursday.

The churches in the town always held an Ecumenical Service on Good Friday morning, meeting in a different place each year. When we were not involved, either with Bob preaching, or worship actually taking place at St Mark's, we went to Shipton. In the early Eighties their Good Friday service was at 9 a.m., but later on it was altered to 10.30 am. Gradually, more and more people from the town made their way up there, until most years it was full, and something 'not to be missed'.

Easter Day arrived, and we always began with an Easter Vigil outside St Mark's at 8 a.m. I can remember when we had drizzle on a couple of occasions, but never rain that was heavy enough to drive us inside. We would have two hymns and some readings and prayers outside before making our way into the Church for the Sermon and Holy Communion. Bob had got Ted Maslin, one of our members, to make us a cross - about 4 - 5 feet high, and cover it with chicken wire; as people arrived for both Services on Easter Morning, they were asked to bring one or two fresh flowers, these were fed through the chicken wire, and slowly the cross was transformed into a blaze of colour. If it was at the right time for daffodils, it would be almost totally yellow; if it was too late, then whatever was in bloom was brought along, and the cross was a multicolour of yellows, pinks and blues. When it was time to move inside, Bob would knock loudly on the door with a walking stick, usually the very stout one that had been his father's (a prized possession) - a Church Steward, alone inside, would open the doors to let people in; the candles of failure would be re-lit, and everyone would follow the candle-bearers to the front as we sang a hymn. Later on, when we had Church banners, the Easter Banner would be held up outside, and then carried in and raised up to be placed on its hook behind the pulpit - I always found that very emotional. I remember one year, when I was a Church Steward, I was sent inside by Bob, to be the "door opener". I was a bit bothered that I might miss my cue, so I put my ear to the heavy oak door to make sure I heard. Bob decided to make sure that I did hear, and hit the door so hard with the stick, just level with my ear - that I nearly jumped out of my skin!

After the 8 a.m. Service, we always had breakfast. Initially this 8 a.m. Communion was the only one that was advertised as a Family Communion, but later on, all 8 a.m. Services became Family Communions and all were followed by breakfast. They were never packed out, but those who experienced them didn't like missing them. And so, as a Church family, we shared Easter Breakfast together. Easter was the only time that we had boiled eggs - courtesy of Ann Blenkinsopp, and her Mum, Joan. Ann later became our Girls Brigade Captain, and to our delight married Stephen Varley who also grew up in the Church, and was a Church Steward.

By 9.45 a.m. everyone had dispersed, to prepare themselves for the 10.30 a.m. Service, usually incorporating Holy Communion, and usually a Family Service. In the evening Bob and I nearly always made our way out to the country, for an Easter Communion with the people of Shipton and Andoversford.

Soon after Easter, Bob and I made our way up to Bedlington, to bring his parents down to Cheltenham for a holiday. We were very amused when, on our way home, having taken a slightly different route, we encountered several stretches of road in the Midlands that were being resurfaced, and suddenly realised that the Pope's visit to that area was within the next week or two. We'd heard of the "red carpet" treatment, but that seemed to be going over and above the call of duty! After two weeks with us, Mum and Dad were going to Epsom to Bob's niece's wedding. Joy is the youngest daughter of Don and Mary. Gillian was married to Pete about 3 days after we returned from Tennessee – in Yorkshire, we were still not acclimatised, but apart from missing the M1 at Leeds on the way home, we made it without mishap! It seems that those girls liked getting married when we were doing Exchanges, because Joy married Roger at the beginning of June, and we left 10 days later, for Ohio.

We had a happy time with Mum and Dad, and then, on the morning of the wedding, Paul and Therese arrived, so that the six of us could travel together. At the last minute Bob decided that we would try to sort out some transport so that we could all be together, rather than hire a car for Paul to drive. He asked Stephen Varley's parents if we could borrow their Volkswagen minibus for the day, and they very kindly agreed; what a difference it made, and what fun we had on the Journey, lots of laughter and wise cracks, but very different from the journey home when we all seemed to have run out of 'steam'.

Mum and Dad stayed on in Epsom for a holiday with Don and Mary and Gillian and Pete, then Don and Mary took them home. We returned home to finish our preparations for our Exchange to Brunswick, Ohio.

Our Exchange partners were Rev Jon Freshwater, his wife Joyce, and two of their sons. We planned to spend a couple of days with them before they left the U.S. for England. Many letters had been exchanged, and the excitement was really beginning to get hold of us by now, and then, suddenly, in the midst of all the last minute washing, on the day before we were due to leave, the washing machine broke down. We were really panicking when we suddenly remembered that we had a repair contract with the Electricity Board, and so friends were organised to get it dealt with before the 'Freshwaters' arrived.

Bright and early on Monday, 14th June 1982, we were at last ready for off, and one of our American friends arrived with her huge [American] station wagon to take us to Heathrow Airport.

Cheltenham is famous for G.C.H.Q. - Government Communications Headquarters - and there are regular visits between people of different nationalities. Carolyn, her husband and daughter, were good friends to us during their time in Cheltenham, and have remained friends ever since. Knowing the family well, she got us organised, and our luggage; and on a beautiful morning, with the early sun shining, lighting up the yellow stone-work of the local village in the unique way that happens only in the Cotswolds, we were off.

Bob found it a rather stressful experience, sitting in the front passenger seat, on the right hand side of the car, in the right hand lane of the M4 - next to the barrier - driving at about 65-70 miles an hour! We reached Heathrow with time to spare, and Carolyn spent time with us as we had some refreshments, and strolled around the airport. When it was time for us to say our goodbyes, she gave us an envelope to be opened on the plane. Once safely on board the T.W.A. 747, we opened the envelope, to find a "Bon Voyage" card and 15 dollars for us to use on the journey. We were really touched by their kindness.

Our 'party' this time consisted of Bob and myself, Rachael, Sarah and my mother. This was to be the first time that Mum had ever left Britain, let alone fly, and she really enjoyed herself. Always after that she spoke as a well-seasoned traveller - "Flying? There's nothing to it, it's smoother than a train!!"

The seven hour flight was smooth, pleasant and uneventful. The service with T.W.A. was excellent, and we all enjoyed it. We had a 6 hour wait at Kennedy Airport, New York, so it didn't bother us that we were delayed a little in Customs. We kept ourselves amused in all sorts of ways; the girls by now were 10 and 7 years, so they were more able to amuse themselves. Rachael, an avid reader, had her head in a book most of the time! And it didn't seem too long before we were on board a 727 bound for Cleveland.

Chapter Eighteen

We were met by Jon and Joyce Freshwater, who gave us a tremendous welcome, and took us to the home of Molly Pfister, who was to accommodate us for two nights, until Jon and Joyce had left for England. Molly's home was spacious and beautiful, and we all enjoyed huge servings of strawberries, cake and ice cream. When we got to the point where we couldn't keep awake any longer, we bade our new friends "good-night" and went to bed.

We had planned a 'lie-in', but Sarah woke early, and had everyone else up. Jon Freshwater arrived, and took us all to 'BIG BOYS' REST-AURANT, where we all ate a huge breakfast. As we arrived at the restaurant, we saw all the posters on the news stands saying that the Falklands War was over; it seemed such a long way away to us now and yet, only two days before, we were caught up with all the news bulletins etc.

We all had a lazy day, but Jon and Bob spent time during the afternoon briefing each other on the situations they were going into, before we all went back to their home for a meal.

Jon and Joyce owned their own home, in Parma Heights, a suburb of Cleveland, about 15 miles from Brunswick. The parsonage had been rented as it was not being used, and so, after our meal, we prepared to travel back to Molly's home. All evening we had been a little concerned to see tornado warnings for our area, flashing up on the T.V. screen, but slowly it became apparent that the danger had passed, and we all made our way to the Freshwaters' Buick (which Bob said was a dream to drive), ready for the drive home. What with the strong wind, country roads, no street lights, a strange car, and driving on the 'wrong' side of the road, I was really very frightened. Bob gave no sign of being bothered, but said afterwards that he hadn't liked it. We heard later, that there had been quite a bit of damage done by the storms, and there were several people lost on Lake Erie.

It was the following evening, after the Freshwaters had left for Cheltenham that we eventually were able to move in, and unpack. That day, according to Bob's diary, was typically English - it rained all day!

The next morning - Thursday, 17th June - was an early start; we had to be at Lakeside, on Lake Erie, in time for lunch. Lakeside is a large Conference Centre, owned by the United Methodist Church of East Ohio; it consists of a large auditorium which seats about 4,000 people, and many homes: some are permanent, usually where people have moved in order to retire; some are 'holiday cottages'; but this particular week of the year, they were all full because it was the week of the Annual Conference for the East Ohio Methodist Church.

We arrived at about 1.00 p.m. That morning the Presiding Bishop - Bishop Thomas - announced that Dave Palmer, the Associate Minister from Brunswick, would introduce Bob to the Conference, but we hadn't arrived! Things were put right at the start of the afternoon session at 2.00 p.m. when he was not only welcomed, but asked to address the 2,000 delegates.

On arrival at Lakeside, we had instructions to find John and Bonnie Youngblood (whom we were certain had Red Indian ancestry; but we were wrong); they were staying with their two children, Johnny and Connie, in holiday accommodation called the "Cherry Pit"; this they had booked without seeing it, and, as it was their first Conference, they didn't know the ropes! It was not luxury by any stretch of the imagination, and the children thought it was "the pits"! Bonnie apparently had spent the whole week saying "And we've got the English Minister and his family coming, what are we going to do?" She needn't have worried; the two families got on well from the very start and have remained firm friends ever since.

We had a delightful 24 hours at Lakeside. During that first afternoon all the Ministers and their wives who had been on Pastoral Exchanges to England, met in the holiday home of Rev Jerry Butcher for "afternoon tea" English style (whatever that is!). We laughed throughout that time together and felt very much at home.

In the evening, Connie looked after Rachael and Sarah, while we went to the Conference Ordination Service. This was a totally new experience for us, and very different from our own Ordination Services. Susan Lausch, a young Minister who grew up at Brunswick United Methodist Church, was to be ordained, which gave our group a great deal of added interest in the proceedings. All were ordained in front of the full Conference, and were supported by their own families, add to this the families of the Delegates and the Conference Centre was full to overflowing; 4,000 people singing hymns of praise is a very moving experience, let alone all the other aspects of that service. At the end, all the Ordinands, their families and friends, went back to the houses in which they were staying, and held a party; so that night there were dozens of parties taking place all over the complex. We went to Susan's party for a short while before going back to the "Cherry Pit" and putting the girls, and ourselves, to bed.

The next morning, we had a lovely breakfast, and a good time talking to Bonnie; it was in discussion with her that we decided to stop at "Cedar Point" on our way back to Brunswick. Cedar Point is a large Amusement Park on the edge of Lake Erie; very similar, in fact, to Six Flags over Georgia, which we experienced in 1978. It cost us $52.50c for all five of us to get in, and all the rides were free; being a hot, sunny day, the weather was perfect for the occasion, although I was badly bitten by insects.

The journey home was broken up by a stop at Huron, and a meal at McDonald's; we had no McDonald's restaurants in Britain at that time so there was great excitement if we ate a meal there! We eventually arrived back at 9.00p.m. - exhausted - only to receive a 'phone message telling Bob to be at the church in Brunswick, 15 miles away, at 7.00 a.m. ready to be taken to the Men's Breakfast Meeting!

Our first Sunday was a wonderful occasion: Brunswick United Methodist Church had two morning services: one at 9.30 a.m., followed by coffee, and then another exactly the same, at 11.00 a.m. We had a tremendous welcome between the two services; and at the end of the morning we were taken to the home of Herb and Ann Meyer for lunch. After a great meal we chatted for a while, and Herb gave us some information on the Amish Settlement in Holmes County, Ohio, which we were planning to visit the next day. It was through this time spent with Herb and Ann that we were able to have use of the United Methodist Minister's Parsonage at Niagara Falls, when we visited later in the Exchange.

Holmes County is about 80 miles south of Brunswick, and the home of the largest Amish community in America, far bigger than Lancaster County in Pennsylvania, and less commercialized. We had been advised to visit the General Store in Charm, which is really just a hamlet but the store sells wonderful Amish quilts, and is less commercialized, and more friendly than those in the larger town of Berlin.

Millers Dry Goods Store in Charm was like stepping into another world; Bob recorded in the diary:

What was perhaps more interesting than the quilts, was the Amish people themselves, for it was like being on a Time Machine that had stopped in the 17th Century. The Amish people use no modern appliances, and the motor car gives way to the horse and buggy in Amish country. They speak English (American version), but when together their native tongue is a German/Dutch dialect. In fact, in their religious services, which are held in different homes, German is spoken. They have strict views, and an austere way of life. Their clothing, horses and buggies are identical, lest pride rule their hearts by dressing differently. I asked if I could photograph an elderly woman in her buggy, but she refused, as did a man who took us on a buggy ride later.

The quilts in the shop were gorgeous, and we treated ourselves to one for our own bed, in turquoise; the girls were treated to a small one each.

The day out was really lovely and Bob records:

A two hour drive back to Parma Heights (where we were living), after a marvellous day out. One of the few on our own during our six-week stay in Brunswick. Turning on the T.V. News at 11.00 p.m., we were delighted to hear of the birth of a Prince. (Prince William)

The next morning turned out to be very wet, so our plans to be out from 10.am to 4.00pm with Rex and Diana Thompson, a young couple from the church, were altered. We went to Duff's Restaurant, a smorgasbord, newly opened in the town; Bob described it in this way:

We had a great variety of things from which to select, and the policy is that you can eat as much or as little as you like. We had a marvellous time there.

Rex and Diana then took us to Hales Farm Settlement which gave us an idea of Ohio life in the early 1800's. As we got to the ticket booth, Rex was asked if we were all one family; Bob, as quick as a flash, said that Rex and Diana were our American cousins, expecting the person in the ticket booth to enjoy the joke; she took him seriously, and entered us all on one family ticket. This became a joke for a long, long time.

Part of the Exchange programme obviously involved "covering" for the Minister; it's true that church life tends to be fairly quiet in the summer and so there is the opportunity for sight-seeing too; but the object of the exercise is to see how the 'other half' live, and to meet the people, forming friendships along the way. So the next day saw Bob visiting patients in hospital in the next town, Medina (pronounced Med-diner); Mum and I at the Women's Circle, and Rachael and Sarah taken by the Church Musical Director, Ardith McLoy to the cinema to see "Bambi". Tea-time saw us at a farewell party for Dave Palmer, the Associate Minister, who was moving to Vermillion, Ohio, to have his own church; this was at the home of Gay and Gerry Vanderzyden, and arranged as a surprise by all the young people of the church. This barbecue/party went on till midnight, but we had to leave at 7.30pm totally amazed at the love these young people had for Dave.

During the winter of 1981/82 Bob and I had joined a beginners group to learn American Square Dancing, and had thoroughly enjoyed ourselves; imagine, then, our delight when we were told that we were going out to supper with some keen square dancers, Ken and Thelma Grove and Jim and Vivian Candrill, and then on to a square dance. When we arrived we met Robert and Eula Brook, also from the church in Brunswick, and also very keen square dancers. We had a wonderful evening and were, almost literally, 'danced off our feet'.

On the Thursday we had called at the Southland Shopping Centre and, for a change, it was Bob who picked up all the bargains: several cheap sports shirts, which he wore every summer until he died, and, what he described as a "J.R. Ewing" hat, after the character in the "Dallas" soap opera. He only paid $3 for it, and it was his pride and joy. Sunday morning worship contained, inevitably, a slot where the hat could be displayed, and this led to a whole range of hats being given to him for his "hat collection" from members of the congregation over the next 6 weeks.

In that congregation on 27th June were Rev Fred Gaston and his wife Margaret. Fred was a retired Methodist Minister, who, at that time lived in Steubenville, Ohio, quite a distance away. He had heard Bob speak at the Conference, and had come, not only to hear him preach, but to ask if we could help him to find accommodation in a typically British Circuit in1983 where he could do some research on British Methodism. Bob and I suggested they use us as their base, and study the Cheltenham Circuit. They did come, and we have remained friends; sadly, Margaret died in the late1980's, but it was a real joy to meet up again when Fred and his new wife, Violet, visited us in Launceston in 1994.

The Gastons wanted to take us out to lunch, but Bob had to take a service in an old people's home, 'Shangri-la', in the afternoon, and we had a packed lunch with us, which we planned to eat at the church; to have travelled the 15 miles back to the house, and then back to Brunswick would have been too time consuming. However, Fred and Margaret didn't mind our rushing off, and so we went back to Duff's. Bob, ever aware of the relatively cheap cost of living in America at that time, compared with Britain, noted it all:

We did go down to Duff's, and had an excellent lunch (eat as much as you liked for a set price), 6 adults for $25 (much better than the bread and butter we'd planned to eat!)

Bob had a good time at 'Shangri-la' and he was asked to go back; one old lady told him "You talk real purdy (pretty)".

During the following week, we received two surprise gifts, both anonymous: one for $40 and with it a note of appreciation; the other tickets for the whole family to go to Sea World (Ohio), worth over $30. Also in that week, we were taken by Linda Duty and her two daughters, Lori and Lana, to the Health Museum in Cleveland. We had never experienced anything like it before, ranging from huge teeth that you could walk inside to displays about sight - we all tested our vision; and much to the delight of the children, a computer that gave you your life expectancy! Grandma filled in the appropriate answers to the set questions, and was told that she could expect to live to her late 60's - she was then 75! The girls thought it hilarious.

On Friday, 2nd July arrangements had been made with Rev Paul Biery, Programmes Director for U.M. Church, Cleveland District, with offices in the 1st U.M. Church, to give us a Methodist tour of the city. The lst Church is a huge building, more like a cathedral, but because it is an inner city church, at that time, only had a congregation of 150 at best. As part of the 'tour' we stopped at the Roman Catholic Cathedral of St John the Evangelist, built about 1920, and very impressive; we went on to Church House, the home of Inter-Church Aid, and we saw how all denominations work together as they tackle the problems of the Inner City. There were literacy programmes which were aimed at helping the 30,000 illiterate people in Cleveland (pop 570,000), and work with the many ethnic minorities, who, in many cases, retain their native languages. We saw Day Care Centres and Hostels: there to meet the needs of all ages; travelled through the Red Light district; had a marvellous lunch in a Polish Restaurant where the Roman Catholic owner's children were all educated in Methodist Schools and Colleges; and were amazed at the number of Greek Orthodox and Russian Orthodox Churches we passed. All in all, it was a very worthwhile visit, and good to see "how the other half live". Our trip was rounded off by a visit to the "Western Shop" to buy Square Dance supplies - shoes for me and shirt and dress patterns too.

Sunday, 4th July was a special day; not just because it was Independence Day but also because Brunswick U.M. Church was welcoming their new Associate Minister - Kevin Roach. The District Superintendent (Dr Bill Weinland), presided at both services, and Bob's preaching was well received. Bob was also amazed at the promises the congregation made to the new Minister, especially the one to 'pay him a fair wage' That morning, he received another hat - a Mexican one this time, and $11 (Canadian) to spend at Niagara during the week.

It was a delight to be included in the 4th July celebrations, and we were taken to the home of Lewis and Roberta Fuller for a family celebration. There were 20 family members there, including the Great Grandmother of 85 years, who spent her early years in Lambeth, London, and although she had lived in the U.S. for more than 60 years, still had a Cockney accent! My Mother had a wonderful time talking to her and also to her brother - their memories going back 60 years were amazing.

Driving back to Parma Heights was quite an experience; fireworks were being let off in every direction - a little like our 5th November, only more so! - This went on into the early hours and Bob recorded it as "a noisy evening".

5th July was a Public Holiday, because 4th July had fallen on a Sunday. We decided to treat ourselves to breakfast at 'Bob's Big Boys Favourite Restaurant'; it was a huge meal, that served us for lunch as well (Brunch). As we returned home, we passed the 'marchers' assembling for the big Independence Day Parade, although we were not around when it actually took place. Our day was rounded off, by a lovely barbecue and fun and games at the home of Gay and Gerry Vanderzyden; we were joined by several families from the church and had a super time together.

2.00 a.m. on 6th July saw the first lunar eclipse since 1736, but we were too tired to stay up and see it; Rachael wanted to but didn't make it. That day turned out to be the hottest day of our trip so far, and one in which we all went our separate ways: Mum and I on a mystery tour, which ended up at Vermillion, Ohio - a really beautiful place on the edge of the lake; the girls spent the day with a church family - the Corrs, who had children of a similar age - and a swimming pool, where they spent most of the day. Bob was busy at the church, making sure all was in order, before we left for our trip to Niagara; during the course of the day he was staggered to discover that the church was paying their minister 3 times more than Bob's stipend, plus many extras!

The next day found us on our way to Niagara Falls; we left at 7.30a.m. and arrived mid-afternoon. We were to stay in the Parsonage of Rev Jim Brewster, who was away on holiday at the time. Herb and Ann Meyer from Brunswick, had lived for 7 years in the town of Niagara, U.S.A., and had contacted the Brewsters on our behalf. We stayed there for 2 nights.

The town of Niagara is very ordinary, and we were very disappointed. We had been advised to see the Falls from the Canadian side first, as the best views are from there, so as soon as possible, we made our way to Rainbow Bridge - the crossing point between the U.S.A. and Canada. Bob was absolutely certain that, as British passport holders, Canada would welcome us with open arms; he was sadly disappointed when he was treated in the same way as everyone else!!

The Falls just took our breath away; spectacular is such an inadequate word to describe the beauty and the power of the Falls. It made us realise once more, that we worship such an amazing and mighty God. We "did" all the traditional tourist sights: a visit to the underground tunnels, where you can view the Falls from just a few feet away; a ride on the 'Maid of the Mist' boat, which takes you very, very close to the torrent of water, pouring over the cliff at hundreds of gallons per second. Bob recorded the event in the diary he kept:

What a picture, to see us all, donned in waterproofs, wellington boots and enjoying, if that's the right word, being so close to the Falls, as not only to hear its noise and feel its power, but to get wet; to ride on 'The Maid of the Mist IV', one of several boats that take the steady stream of visitors up river to the bottom of the Falls, and to feel the spray of water. A marvellous experience, not to be missed.

At 9.15 p.m. we made our way back to the Falls, to see the lights come on, lighting up the different sections in the colours of the rainbow – all that is except the 'Bridal Veil Falls', a comparatively small water fall, which was shown up in white.

On our first Exchange to Tennessee, one of our friends referred to gift shops as "Currency Removal Joints"; Bob often quoted him! He notes in the diary of an 'obligatory' visit to the Currency Removal Joints of Niagara, but doesn't note, that he enjoyed wandering around them too - as long as it didn't take up too much time!

The next morning saw us back in Canada, to visit the Niagara Falls Museum, where amongst other things, we saw accounts of man – and woman's - many attempts to travel over the Falls in every sort of capsule that you can imagine. We drove into Canada and had lunch in a small town called 'Niagara on the Lake', and enjoyed a little of Canada before travelling back and viewing the Falls from the American side. It was much more attractive than we had been led to believe, and there were virtually no Currency Removal Joints!

The next day, we were back to 'normal'; arriving back to find that there had been three deaths during our three days away, but all had been taken care of by the Associate Minister, Kevin Roach.

Sunday 11th July was rather different to the others; Bob acted as 'Liturgist" (worship leader), and I preached. Both the 9.30 a.m. and the 11 a.m. services were the same, so we had a good go at it! Bob introduced me by saying that I was a fully qualified Lay Preacher, and that this was an unpaid job, unlike the Minister; going on to say that "I get paid for being good, she's good for nothing!" That evening, we had a service of Holy Communion - English style, many people expressed their appreciation.

Monday, 12th July dawned, and we left on a 400 mile trip to Washington D.C. The journey was glorious, and took us through beautiful forests and across the Allagheny Mountains. We were to stay with Don and Brenda Thomas - Brenda originally came from Cheltenham, and had met Bob when he conducted a relative's funeral; they had only just arrived (due to Brenda's work) but made us very welcome. It was good to meet up with Don and Betsy Pulcifer for a meal - they had spent three years in Cheltenham (where we met them), and had just arrived back.

We packed as much as we could into our visit to Washington, the next day we took the 'Tourmobile' as it was easier on the feet – especially Mum's; and generally saw most of the sights that we saw in 1978, mainly because it was Mum's first visit. As before, we found the Kennedy graves most moving, but didn't have enough time to spend on all the things we wanted to see. Going home, we experienced the Washington rush hour, and vowed to never experience it again - if possible!

We travelled home on 14th July (Wed.), and chose a route that took us via Gettysburg. Bob records:

A stop at Gettysburg, Pennsylvania, proved worthwhile; and we were quite amazed, not only at the significance of the place, but the way in which one of the important areas of the American Civil War of 1862-1865, has been preserved. Monuments abound, of the many different soldiers, serving their own particular State, but adding up to some 55,000 casualties from both the North and the South. Gettysburg was not only an historic scene of death and destruction; for it was here, late in 1863, after the Battle, that President Abraham Lincoln delivered his famous speech of hope; honouring the dead of both sides, he concluded... We here, highly resolve that these dead, shall not have died in vain; and that, government of the people, by the people, for the people, shall not perish from the earth.

We were all very impressed by Gettysburg, and were glad that we stopped for as long as we did.

The following weekend was very different; the girls stayed with friends for the weekend - the Youngbloods and the Vanderzydens; Bob was on his own and Mum and I were part of a seven women delegation from Brunswick, at the United Methodist Women of East Ohio Conference, meeting at Mount Union College, Alliance, Ohio. The Saturday was the annual United Methodist Day at the Baseball Stadium in Cleveland, home of the Cleveland Indians. Bob was taken there by Al Lausch; and at the 'Behind the Fence Party' he met up with Bishop Thomas - President (Bishop) of the Conference. Bob, Mum and I had met him when we stopped off at his office in Canton, on our way to Alliance, and Bob was delighted to see this charming man again. The Bishop threw the first ball of the game, and although the Indians were losing for much of the game, they eventually won 10-4, in their match against the California Angels.

The Sunday morning held a wonderful surprise. During the morning, someone left a large parcel in the study at the church; the card told us it was a gift from Jim and Vivienne Caudill, Ken and Thelma Grove and Robert and Eula Brook - the friends who had been taking us Square Dancing. The gift was a Square Dance outfit for us both - matching yellow and brown; we just couldn't believe it, and felt so privileged to have been sent to that Church.

Fairly early on in our Exchange, we had been given an anonymous gift of tickets for the family to visit Sea World. We went on the Monday (l9th July), and had a wonderful time, but would have spent a lot longer there if time had allowed. The Seal and Otter Show was a great hit with all the family, and we went back to see it again, at the end of our visit. Shamu - the killer whale was good; fortunately we were seated away from the area where he splashed his tail, soaking the crowd nearby! We also enjoyed the Dolphin show.

The Japanese Section was beautiful; for a payment of $6.40, a pearl diver would dive for an oyster with the guarantee of a pearl! An offer which we did not take up! We finished off the day with a meal at McDonald's, and then the girls left with their friends, the Vanderzydens. This gave Bob, Joy and Mum, the opportunity to go to the cinema to see "Chariots of Fire", newly released and highly acclaimed. The diary records: 'We felt extremely patriotic and VERY British!!'

This week was Vacation Bible School, a holiday club run by the Church; the girls were keen to be involved, and thoroughly enjoyed it, and we popped in and out. Once more, we were taken Square Dancing, this time on the edge of Lake Erie at a place called Bay Village; Mum and the girls came with us and enjoyed watching us.

The next day, Terry Paquin, one of Brunswick Church's members, took us all to the outdoor theatre at New Philadelphia where we were to see the presentation "Trumpet in the Land", We went via East Liverpool where Terry had friends, and we enjoyed a lovely meal with Mr & Mrs Curry.

The drama production was 2½ hours long and about the missionary activities of the Moravian Church in 1782. This was under the influence of Peter Bohler, the Moravian leader, who made such a great impact on the life of John Wesley in 1738. The backdrop was a natural hillside, and the first characters to appear came on horseback, over the hill; we were most impressed, and had a wonderful evening.

The East Ohio Conference each year collected a large group of young people together to give a presentation of music and testimony, which for several weeks in the summer, was taken on a tour of Churches throughout the Connexion - I'm not sure if they still do it. It was a great thrill for any teenager to be chosen to be part of that group; there were lots of rehearsals, and several weekends away, in order that the young people were ready to give a polished performance; every one of them was expected to give their testimony at some time during the tour. We were privileged to be taken to see "Youth Musicalle", when one of the three groups that were travelling in 1982 performed one night at the Methodist Church in Medina, just down the road from Brunswick; they were excellent, and we all thoroughly enjoyed the evening; even now, we still occasionally play the tape of the music.

Our six weeks Exchange drew to a close, and we had our last service at the church on Sunday, 25th July. The two morning services were well attended, and there were some emotional farewells, even though there was to be an 'official' Church Picnic from 2 p.m.-7 p.m. in which our goodbyes could be said.

The picnic was a delightful occasion, with lots of good food and time to talk and play; Bob played volleyball and tried to master, unsuccessfully, soft ball. The children were involved in everything that was going. At 6.30 p.m., the teenagers led us in vespers; this was followed by the official words of farewell, and many gifts, my mother was given the newly published book by Robert Lacey, of the Royal Wedding; this delighted her. I was given a picture of the Resurrection of Jesus and a beautiful tissue box cover in the shape of a house. Bob was given a clock for the 'Pastor's Study' with a verse engraved on it and a commemorative plaque. Bob concludes this part of the diary, with the words:
> Farewells were moving and sad; but we were extremely happy at having thrown ourselves into the work of Brunswick Church.

As we left the picnic, Bob managed to lock the car (with the automatic locking system) with the keys inside and the engine running! Panic ensued for a while, but fortunately, someone managed to open the door with the aid of a cooking utensil!! Bob wrote that night:
> The Exchange was over; but we had had a wonderful time, and had made many 'new' friends.

The rest of the evening was busy; we dropped off some suitcases ready packed for London, at the Youngbloods, and packed the rest of our belongings to take with us to Etowah, Tennessee, the place of our first Exchange in 1978.

Chapter Nineteen

At 7.20 a.m. on 26th July, the day after our farewell picnic, one of the Brunswick members, Dick Beeching, arrived to take us to Etowah; he had offered to drive us the 550 miles, and we were delighted to accept, and so our 3 weeks holiday began.

The journey took 12 hours, and Dick and Bob shared the driving. On arrival at our friends Matney and Mildred Reed's, we were given a wonderful meal, but were a little concerned that Dick intended to drive straight back; he insisted he would be O.K., and said he had done it before, so we could do no more than thank him, profusely, for his kindness, and wave him off.

Meeting Matney and Mildred after 4 years was wonderful; it was as if we had only been apart for a couple of days; we just picked up where we'd left off. Unfortunately, Mildred was suffering, quite badly, from shingles, and so the plan to stay there had been revised, and we were given the use of the basement flat in Mrs Graham's house, just a few yards up the road from the Methodist Church. She made us very welcome, and we found that the refrigerator was filled with goodies including: a home roasted ham, bacon, eggs, cantaloupe melons (our favourite), pancakes, syrup - all gifts from some other dear friends - Kathleen Watson and her sister Irene.

The next day we went to visit Kathleen and Irene, and were given a belated Christmas gift - $100 in a beautiful card.

Matney had made a car available to us for the whole of the three weeks; It was a very large Chrysler automatic, quite old, but wonderful to ride in - Bob felt like a king when he drove it! It had a bench seat in the front - a new experience for three of us to be in the front at times! Matney and Mildred are avid square dancers and the next evening, we were taken by Matney to Cleveland, Tennessee to a Square Dance where we had a lovely time. Mildred didn't feel up to it, but took Mum, Rachael and Sarah to the nearby town of Athens to see the film 'E.T.', unfortunately there were long queues and the cinema was full, long before they got to the box office. On the Thursday (29th July), they did manage to see the film, while Matney took Bob and me to the Square Dance Club at the Methodist Church (St Paul's) in Etowah.

It was only natural that the girls would want to show Grandma the places they remembered from our first Exchange, and so we were soon off to Chatanooga. We had a ride up Lookout Mountain on the Incline Railway – the steepest railway in the world. Four years before, we had driven the car up, and by the end of the day, wished we had done so again! We hadn't realised that the top of the mountain is, in fact a plateau of 83 miles, with parts in Tennessee, Georgia and Alabama, and so we had to wait for a bus, which took us on a half hour journey to Rock City, We really enjoyed this second visit, and the girls delighted in showing us all the places they could remember. Our trip back to the incline was ok, but on arrival, we discovered that it was out of order, and after a long wait, were taken down the mountain by bus, via Rock City - the place we had just left!

We were late arriving at the Chatanooga Choo Choo Station, where we were to meet Matney, Mildred and their daughter, Rebecca; but they were still there. We had our meal in the restaurant - a treat from the Reed's and especially so for the girls - they didn't get treats like that in England! And then the obligatory photos on the Choo Choo train - Bob never managed to get his taken there, but only complained when we were back in England, and it was too late!

The journey home was via Allamande Hall, a large, purpose built hall for square dancing, and we spent a while watching the dancers. The keen interest in square dancing had grown since our last visit, because Bob and I had joined a club in Cheltenham about 18 months before.

The Saturday saw us all at the picnic area of Quinn Springs, by the Hiwassee River for breakfast; this event lasted until 11 a.m. We were the guests of the Reeds, Dwight and Grace McKay, J.E. and Viola Watson, and Kathleen and Irene, and a wonderful time was had by all. We went on from the picnic area to Reliance, a small community that has grown up around the bridge over the river - the General Store there is unique, and sells virtually anything you could name and from there we went on alone; crossing the river, and making our way up to the Power House on the river.

At certain times of the day, the power company release hundreds of tons of water from the storage dam and many people 'raft' down the river on this 'tidal' wave. We had, by accident chosen the right time, and watched people ride down the river in canoes, inner tubes and any other sort of craft they could lay their hands on; men, women and children all seemed to be having a wonderful time, but I wasn't so sure that it was my kind of event!

Sunday 1st August was a red-letter day. All the family, except Grandma, were involved in the Worship Service at St Paul's United Methodist Church, Etowah, that morning. I was Liturgist; the girls, Acolytes which meant that they were responsible for the lighting and extinguishing of the candles on the Communion Table - and Bob preached. The girls processed in, dressed in cassocks, looked lovely, and behaved beautifully; the congregation were delighted with the Wilson contribution.

On a return visit to Gatlinburg, at the foot of the Smokey Mountains, we walked into a candle shop, and straight into a family whose faces were familiar; they turned out to be Rev John Mitchell, Chairman of the Newcastle-Upon-Tyne District, on Exchange, with his family in Birmingham, Alabama. Gatlinburg is a typical tourist resort, it is an ideal place for buying souvenirs to take home. Etowah is not particularly geared up to tourists and we could do most of our gift shopping in one fell swoop. This time we took the lift to the top of the Space Needle, and it was well worth the trip ~ the views were absolutely spectacular.

One morning, Matney dropped by to suggest we take a trip together to McKamy Lake; 3,000 feet up into the mountains in the Cherokee National Forest, and about 45 minutes drive away. The lake is man-made, and surrounded with imported sand - the nearest thing to the seaside we could find. We had enjoyed an afternoon there in 1978, and were looking forward to the return visit. We took 'our' car, and Bob drove; he frightened Matney to death when, after a stop in a lay-by to admire the view, he started to drive on the wrong side of the road on a blind bend!! Matney just couldn't get the words out quickly enough, but Bob did get the message and pulled over before any vehicles came along. The day spent there was lovely, and we swam and sunbathed, but, as often happened, Bob overdid it, and burned himself badly. That night we went back to Allamande Hall to a Square Dance, but Bob's sunburn began to affect him. All the square dancers were pleased to see us - it was quite a novelty to have dancers from England.

On Sunday, 8th August, we left straight after morning service, to go to Knoxvllle and in particular, to visit the World's Fair. We ate sandwiches in the car to save time, and we managed to park our car just a few blocks away from the entrance, so we were walking around before we knew it. Our entrance tickets were gifts from Kathleen Watson, and it was a real delight to be there.

Sunday proved to be a good day, with not too many crowds. Our first stop was at the Chinese exhibit; many people had told us how impressed they were with this, but it did not do the same for us, as we had seen similar things in the U.K.; we were all rather amused, though, when Sarah, then aged 7, announced that she thought the Chinese exhibit was "excellent". The American exhibit was by far the largest, and that, along with the Japanese, appealed more to the girls than any other. By contrast, the British exhibit was minute! Our national pride came out as we slowly made our way around, looking at sections about the Children's T.V programme "Blue Peter"; a British Leyland 'Metro' car; a coal mining exhibit, complete with pit props made by 'Dowty' a Cheltenham firm; but the crowds were all fighting for a front row position to watch a video of the wedding of Prince Charles and Lady Diana Spencer - we grew rather annoyed with my mother, who was also dying to get to the front, and she had seen it over and over again on British TV!

As we continued to walk around, the heavens opened and it poured with rain, but it didn't deter the weather-hardened British; we carried on regardless! We took time to watch the Clydesdale horses and were dragged on to "The Log Ride" – Bob reckoned that they got more wet from the rain than the ride in an imitation log, through a long channel of water with lots of ups and downs.

Two days later, after filling the car with 22.2 gallons (U.S.A. = 6 pints to 1 gallon) of petrol, at a cost of $25 - remarkably cheap, compared with England, we were on our way to Lake Junaluska, to re-visit the conference centre that we had enjoyed so much In 1978. The journey was glorious and took us through the Smokey Mountains; we took our time and arrived at 4 p.m. We dropped our luggage in our room, and went to see Dr & Mrs Wright Spears, the parents of our dear friend, Mary Ann Brockwell; the girls were delighted to see their small poodle - Happy ~ and played continuously with her. From there, we made our way to the Cokesbury Bookshop, named after Thomas Coke and Francis Asbury, two of the early Methodist preachers from England, who made a tremendous impact on American society in the 18th Century. These 'bookshops' sell you anything you could possibly want in church life; from church furniture to cassocks, to jewellery, ornaments, Sunday school equipment, as well as books and Bibles. We always spent too much money in the Cokesbury Shops!!

That evening, we drove to Asheville, North Carolina, about a half hour's drive away, and met up with Matney and Mildred Reed, at the home of Matney's two very elderly aunts. After a lovely time with them, the Reeds took us to the Biltmore Dairy Bar - part of the famous Biltmore estate, we all enjoyed delicious ice creams; we felt as if we were in a film, the setting was just as we see portrayed in productions of the 1940's, and a very different experience for us.

The next morning was spent playing shuffle board, visiting the memorial Chapel, the Susanna Wesley Gardens, and the World Methodist Council Building where we saw the Travelling Pulpit, used by John Wesley, and many of the famous portraits of our Methodist ancestors.

From there, we made our way down Maggie Valley, through the most glorious scenery, and into the town of Cherokee, arriving at about 1 p.m; we did quite a bit of shopping in the Indian Co-operative where, Bob records

Prices were quite high, but where we could at least buy authentic Indian goods.

We made our way back to Etowah, via Gatlinburg, although this time we didn't stop!

11.30 a.m. next morning saw us on the road again, this time to Helen, Georgia; Ethel Loftis and her daughter, Debbie, picked us up and took us back to this delightful town at our request. The route took us through some glorious scenery, and much of it followed the Ocoee River (pronounced O-coy) and Parksville Lake - the river was full of 'rafters', once again, riding on inner tubes as well as in canoes and inflatables.

Helen was crowded, and the temperatures in the 90's; but we enjoyed being there; the town seemed to have been improved since we were there four years before, and there were many more German, Bavarian, Swiss and Alpine buildings and shops. Believe it or not, we were back in Etowah for 9.30p.m and called in at the church for the last half hour of the Church Square Dance Club - the Etowah Sugarfooters; we were presented with their badges with our names on - a square dance tradition; and also a letter telling us that Bob and I were now honorary members of the Club.

Our last full day in Etowah was spent visiting our many friends, and saying some very emotional goodbyes; further farewells were said at

Church the next morning, and after lunch at the Reeds', we left, with them, for Knoxville Airport, to pick up our rental car. Once more, we found it hard to say goodbye to Matney and Mildred, our bonds of friendship, now even closer, but we were all optimistic that it would not be too long before we were together again; although, as it happened, it was to be 10 years until we met, this time in England. The first stage of our journey was to Louisville, Kentucky, to meet and stay the night with our friends, Charles and Mary Ann Brockwell; the journey through the Cumberland Mountains was, once more, spectacular. Our stay was literally overnight, arriving at 7.45 p.m. on the Sunday night and leaving at 9 a.m. on the Monday morning, but it was lovely to see them again.

Stage two was just over 300 miles, and took us through the cities of Cincinnati and Columbus, Ohio, and on to Brunswlck. A tremendous welcome awaited us, not least from the Youngblood family, but also from other church families who dropped in, many bringing gifts and a lovely sketch of the family, done by Bob Lewis about 20 inches by 28 inches, it has pictures of each member of the family and contains the message: ".. and so the lives of many have been touched ..."

The next day now with 10 suitcases - considerably more than we arrived with, and all given by friends - we set off for Hopkins Airport, Cleveland, along with John, Bonnie, Johnny and Connie Youngblood; Jerry and Gay Vanderzyden and their children: Chris, Heidi, Heather and Jerry; and Dick Beeching and his children too. As the plane took off, Rachael was sobbing her heart out, this continued for most of the way to New York! We had 2 - 3 hours to wait at Kennedy Airport, so Bob and Grandma changed their dollars into English money while we waited; Bob comments

which meant that Joy was restricted in her spending in the Airport gift shops.

This delighted him!

We landed at Heathrow at 7.30 a.m. on Wednesday, 17th August. As we left Customs we were surprised and delighted to see Joy's brother's wife Mary, with the children, Anne and Mark, waiting to see us and welcome us home. We chatted together for a while before Rodney Langston and Stan Collins, members from Andoversford Methodist Church, arrived with the Scout minibus - our chauffeurs for the journey home. We had a stop for refreshments on the way, and Bob was staggered at the prices of hamburgers etc, compared with America -

Cheeseburger and Chips U.K. = £2.10 and 35p, the same in the U.S. = 40p and 30p!!! To be fair, this was not comparing McDonalds U.S. with McDonalds U.K. so not a true comparison.

As we arrived at the manse, not only was our friend Penny Campbell, waiting for us, but Paul had come down from Birmingham to see us - what a lovely surprise! Penny had prepared a lovely lunch and her husband, Mike joined us during his lunch hour.

Bob closed the diary with the words:
The Exchange was over, but we had had a marvellous time, and thank God for His goodness, and the privilege which was ours as a family. We had made many "new" friends, and our experience had been enriched in so many different ways.

Chapter Twenty

Our fourth year in the Cheltenham Circuit began with great enthusiasm and eagerness to share all we had experienced in the U.S. Our 'settling in' period was well and truly over and we felt at home. Bob had found his niche in the Ministry, and loved our churches and the Circuit in Cheltenham, and they loved him. After a long period of searching, he had learned to be himself and from that point on his ministry started to change and it became more meaningful to himself and everyone around him.

The girls had settled well both into school life and church life, and Grandma too found a role within St Mark's and the women's groups especially. My preaching was becoming ever more satisfying, and I found myself taking an increasingly greater role within Bob's ministry - our lives had truly become a partnership in every sense of the word.

In 1983, we said a sad farewell to our American friends, Carolyn and Calvin Scholl, and their young daughter, Dawn. They had worshipped at St Mark's for three years, and we had become friends, sharing meals together, and especially Thanksgiving Dinners in their home. As they prepared to leave, we made the decision to cancel our planned Exchange for 1984, and to use the Scholls as our base for a holiday, instead.

The summer of 1983 was spent with Margaret and Fred Gaston, from Ohio; (we had met them during our Exchange of 1982). They spent a month with us, cramming as much information (and visits) into that time as was humanly possible to do. They probably knew more about British Methodism than we did by the time they had finished! During the Gaston's time with us, the Methodist Conference met in Middlesbrough and Bob made arrangements for them to go; it was difficult to sort out transport because of the timings, so Bob drove them up, had lunch and drove back; he was exhausted by the time he got home! Two days later, he was rushed into hospital with a violent nosebleed that wouldn't stop; he was kept in for three days and we were relieved that we had said our goodbyes to the Scholls the night before! There seemed no reason for the nosebleed, and it was assumed that he had overdone it.

It was a hectic summer, but it gave us a good excuse to tour the local sights, visit local chapels, and learn some new things about the Cotswolds and John Wesley. We also took Margaret and Fred to the New Room in Bristol, the oldest Methodist Preaching Place in the world; and to Oxford, to visit Lincoln College, where John Wesley was a Fellow, even to the extent of seeing his room there!

The morning we said goodbye to Margaret and Fred also saw us preparing to go on our own holiday to Grange-over-Sands; we were able to obtain low-priced accommodation there, and it became, over the years, a favourite place for all the family.

September arrived, and a new Methodist year began, and we also began to make our plans for our holiday in America, the following summer. We wanted to visit all our friends, so we planned to hire a car, and do a circular tour, leaving from Maryland, going on to Ohio, Kentucky and then to Tennessee; unfortunately, as it turned out, Matney and Mildred Reed were going to be away at that time, so Tennessee was dropped from the itinerary.

This time, we were to fly from Gatwick, and Rodney Langston, the friend who picked us up from Heathrow in 1982, had agreed to take us to and from the airport; he had no car at the time, and so it worked very well; we drove to his home, left the car with him, and he used it while we were away. He managed to get permission to use the minibus from the school where he worked - ideal for all our luggage!

We were eager to go to America in 1984, to feel part of the Bicentenary of American Methodism. Lovely Lane United Methodist Church is in Baltimore, and we wanted to be as close to there as possible; Carolyn and Cal had pointed out, that if we were sent to the wrong side of Chesapeake Bay it would cost us an awful lot of money in travelling expenses. The Scholls lived in Severna Park, between Washington and Baltimore, an ideal place to be based; hence our change of plans a year earlier.

Once more we planned to take Grandma, and we began to look forward to seeing old friends again. Bob had offered to preach each Sunday, and was delighted to have the opportunity to take a service in the Lovely Lane Church, which is known as the "Mother Church of American Methodism." It was founded in a simple meeting house in 1784, but the original was replaced by a much grander building, to celebrate its centenary in 1882.

We left England when the girls finished school for the summer, and flew directly to Maryland; to the Baltimore/Washington International Airport. It was good to see the Scholl family once more and Dawn, Rachael and Sarah just picked up where they left off; in fact, we all did.

In the first few days we were taken by Carolyn to get the feel of the area and this included an introductory look at the Lovely Lane Church (and the museum in the basement), in preparation for Bob's preaching appointment there on the Sunday.

We learned that in December 1784, the Lovely Lane Meeting House hosted an important meeting of Methodist preachers (the "Christmas Conference"), which resulted in the founding of the Methodist Episcopal Church in the United States of America. The present building [which is on a different site] that houses the Lovely Lane Methodist Church was designed by Stanford White in 1882 as a Centennial Monument to the founding of American Methodism. By the mid-1970s, the church had fallen into disrepair and the turn-of-the-century heating and electrical systems had become inadequate. A large-scale renovation was undertaken in the 1980s to fix the problems and modernize the church.

The building is beautiful, but the ceiling is amazing: it's painted with a depiction of the sky exactly as it appeared at 3:00 a.m. the day of the church's dedication, with all the major stars and planets in their proper positions.

The original church was formed in 1771; Francis Asbury, founder of American Methodism was its first Minister, and served there several times. He is almost more revered in the U.S. than Wesley himself. Born in the Midlands, he left England when he was in his 20's, in response to Wesley's plea that more people were needed for the work in America, - he never returned home!

Sunday, 29th July 1984 was a glorious day, and we had a wonderful time of worship with the members of the Lovely Lane Church. Bob preached on the Grace of God. The Scholls came with us, and when the 10 a.m. service was over, and we were ready to leave, we were taken by Carolyn and Cal to Baltimore Harbour, now transformed into an attractive leisure area. They also took us for a brief look at other historical sights; at a later visit we took in more of the Baltimore area, including Fort McHenry, whose forces in 1814, defeated the British Fleet. This story was told to us with great delight, but Rachael, then aged 12, didn't appreciate it! It was during this battle that the words of the U.S. National Anthem "The Star Spangled Banner" were written.

During the week we made our way south to Ohio; stopping firstly, at the home of Margaret and Fred Gaston in Stuebenville, Ohio. It was good to see them again, and we stayed two nights with them; they took us on a memorable visit to Wheeling Zoo, in West Virginia, and we also enjoyed seeing the presentation they had put together about English Methodism.

From Stuebenville, we moved on to Brunswick, Ohio, where we had taken part in an Exchange of pulpits in 1982. It felt as if we had never been away. It was good to meet Tom Hampton and his family; he had been writing to us for two years, having enjoyed our ministry in 1982, but we couldn't picture him at all, the friendship has stood the test of time, and we are still in touch. On Sunday morning - 9.30 a.m. and 11 a.m. - Bob preached on the "Five Alls". Taking the name of a pub in Cheltenham, he enlarged on its theme: I govern all; I pray for all; I plead for all: I fight for all; I pay for all.

We moved on to Louisville, Kentucky, and spent two nights with our friends, Charles and Mary Ann Brockwell; during that time we were taken to Lincoln's Birthplace, and drove past Fort Knox. We first met Charles and Mary Ann at Lake Junaluska in 1978; over the years we have spent time with each other, sometimes in our home and sometimes in theirs. Mary Ann is a teacher and Charles both a Methodist minister, an historian and a Professor at Louisville University. Their memories of Bob are precious to me, because they remember him both as a minister and as a friend. After Bob's death, Charles wrote:

Something special about Bob that I remember is his sermon register. The neat, handwritten entries of texts for years of Sundays, demonstrated a devotion to the office of Preacher of the Word, that is unique in my experience of preachers. I was doubly impressed because he kept this record, not only of his sermons, but included his guest preachers as well. It is a source of inspiration to me to think about being in 'Bob's register'. It bound me, and still binds me to him, in the Word. It keeps me reminded when I preach that I am a member of a kerygmatic brotherhood/sisterhood all round the world.

Then I remember Bob's love for all his family. It seemed to me that he rejoiced in each one, for the special interests and gifts that person has. Above all, I remember how proud he was of you!

[Joy] Love and respect were interwoven when he spoke of you, or of your life together.

We left Louisville and made our way, through West Virginia, to Cumberland Gap, where we stayed the night at the Holiday Inn. Friends told us to stay at the Holiday Inn, because the prices were reasonable, and you "know what you're getting!" We drove around, and tried to find a cheaper place, but gave up in the end; the hotel had a swimming pool, and the girls spent the whole evening in there; Sarah had not been too well, and it was good to see her relax.

We arrived back at Severna Park in time for an evening meal on the Friday, and Bob prepared himself for the service (at 10 a.m.) on Sunday, 12th August 1984 at Severna Park United Methodist Church, where he preached once more on the "Five Alls".

We spent our final 10 days with the Scholl family, visiting all the local places of interest, not least - the craft shops - both Carolyn and I spent hours in them - and a small fortune in money! One of our most impressive visits was to Annapolis, home of the United States Naval Academy. We were disappointed that the Chapel was closed for a wedding, and so we went back on the Monday morning - two days before our flight home. We arrived at 9 a.m. on a glorious morning, the Chapel looked wonderful, but as we stepped inside, the organist was practising and we were transported to heaven.

Our fourth Sunday was spent in Bowie (pronounced Boowy), Maryland, with our friends, Don and Betsy Pulcilpher, who had been in Cheltenham for three years during the late seventies and early eighties. Bob preached at their church - St Matthew's United Methodist Church, Bowie, this time on "Priorities". His text was taken from 1 Corinthians 1:1-17. He began by referring to the divisions at Corinth, and saying how important it is to support each other; he used this illustration: (adapted for the U.S. listeners):

As you know, I'm keenly interested in football - although I am now too old to participate. When asked what football team I support I always say, I support "United". Firstly, I support Newcastle United, and the reason? For 28 years I lived on Tyneside, and every young boy was weaned on soccer. Secondly, I support Leeds United, in my opinion the finest Club side in the world. Two main reasons why I support Leeds United. Firstly, I spent three years in a Methodist Theological College in Leeds, and the first four years of my ministry in the West Riding of Yorkshire. The second reason why I support Leeds United, is the fact that Jack Charlton worked in the same pit at Ashington, Northumberland - of course he left when he was 17 and has played for Leeds United for 20 years. And then there's Manchester United. The reason - Bobby Charlton, brother to Jack, has served them, and his country, for many years. So if you ask me who I support, I answer 'United' and keep you guessing!

Bob also supported Watford, but not having the word 'united' in its name, it didn't fit the illustration!!

We moved on to verse 17 "For Christ did not send me to baptize, but to preach the Gospel, and not with eloquent wisdom, lest the cross of Christ be emptied of its power", and to his own ordination:

I can take you back to 18th June, 1968. The place: Wesley's Chapel, City Road, London. The event: the ordination of a number of young ministers, at the end of their 6 year period of training....

What took place on 18th June 1968, when Gordon Rupp, the then President of Conference, laid his hands upon me, had its origins many years before, when a young miner of 22 responded to the preaching of the Gospel, and gave his life to the Lord Jesus Christ. The preaching of the Gospel, or the word of the Cross, runs through Paul's letters, like a golden thread. But of course, when Paul speaks of the Cross, he was not thinking of the actual piece of wood, nor was the word of the Cross simply the story of the crucifixion in all its gruesome details, It was the glad news that "God was in Christ, reconciling the world unto himself". It was the message about what this event meant for man's redemption. Of God doing something for us, which we could never do for ourselves. Paul knew this as a real experience; one which changed the course of his life, and he never grew tired of reminding his hearers, that this supreme event was for them as well.......Because of what Jesus has done, we remain forever debtors to our God....

When Paul talked of Christ not sending Him to baptize, but to preach the Gospel, Paul was, in effect, getting his priorities right - perhaps we would see a difference, if ministers and preachers were released... and we could say ... Christ did not send me to

*be an administrator, or a fund-raiser, but to preach the Gospel;
then I believe we might see a transformation in the effectiveness
of our work and witness.*

For the U.S.A. Bob had a new introduction:
*You've probably heard the story of two members of a certain
church who were discussing the sermon which the preacher had
just delivered. The first member said 'I thought the sermon was
divine, it reminded me of the peace of God. It passed all
understanding!'*

*The second member: 'I believe it reminded me of the mercies of
God. I thought it would endure for ever.'*

*In the five services at which I've preached this past month, I've
noticed that in each case the Offertory or Collection was taken
immediately after the Sermon. No doubt you're familiar with the
well-known story of a preacher who announced to his
congregation, one beautiful Sunday morning 'My good people, I
have in my hands three sermons: a $100 sermon that lasts 5
minutes; a $50 sermon that lasts 15 minutes; and a $10 sermon
that lasts a full hour. Now, we'll take the collection, and see which
one you want me to deliver'.*

Bob closed by saying:
*We return to England on Thursday morning and a week later, we'll
attend a ceremony in the little village of Pill on the river Avon, near
Bristol; when a marker will be unveiled, commemorating Francis
Asbury's departure from England on 4th September, 1771. Earlier
in the summer, at a Conference held in the New Room in Bristol
(opened in 1739), John Wesley had asked the question 'Our
brethren in America call aloud for help, who are willing to go over
and help them?' Francis Asbury was one of those who responded
positively... The Gospel lesson ... comes across the centuries
with the same challenge ....'No-one can serve two masters - you
cannot serve God and Mammon'.*

*Many of you are my age, middle-aged and over, and will
remember the film 'A man called Peter', which portrayed the life
and ministry of the Rev Peter Marshall ... one of his favourite texts
was: 'Seek ye first the kingdom of God', and these words are
addressed to us all.*

What are the priorities of Christian people; seeking first the kingdom of God, but what does that mean in reality? Let me offer you my interpretation:

PRIORITIES Top of the list:

WORSHIP What we do here on a Sunday morning, is the most important thing of all.

FELLOWSHIP (Bible study, discussions, prayer etc.)

SERVICE Methodists have always believed that we were raised up, by God, to spread scriptural Holiness; and you interpret that, not in the kind of piety that evokes the criticism 'Too heavenly minded to be any earthly good'. Holiness for Methodists is expressed in practical ways, as duty to God and our fellow men: here, and throughout the whole wide world.

A top priority for any preacher is faithfulness to the demands of the Gospel, and its proclamation. For everyone else - including the preacher - is the responsibility to

LIVE THE GOSPEL - that in all we do and say and think, the name of Jesus Christ is glorified.

That we are people (young and old), who have ceased to do what we want to do, and have begun to do what Jesus wants us to do. AMEN.

We enjoyed our final days in the Scholl's home, and prepared to return to England. We knew it would be a while before we would be able to 'splash out' on another trip, unfortunately, that was not to be during Bob's lifetime.

Our flight home was good, and once more, Rod Langston was there to meet us; once again he had the mini-bus so all fitted in easily. Sarah spent the whole flight, sitting next to the window, with the blind down! Insisting she was not bothered by flying!!

Chapter Twenty One

Less than a week after our return, Bob's father was diagnosed with a gangrenous leg which was immediately amputated; he never really recovered from it, and died within two weeks. We had known he was unwell, but hadn't realised how ill he was, and so, unfortunately, we didn't get to see him. Bob's mum found it hard, having lost Edna less than three years before.

That September, Bob had been asked to take the Harvest Service at Bedlington Colliery Methodist Church, and the girls and I went up for the weekend. We had agreed to bring Mum back to Cheltenham with us, and she stayed for two weeks before moving on to Epsom to stay with Gill and Pete, and Joy and Roger - Bob's nieces. Don and Mary were down there, waiting for Don's heart by-pass operation, and it was probably the last time she spent any time with them.

Our trip to America really re-vitalised us in every way, not least spiritually; we really wanted to roll up our sleeves and get on with the work. Our Christmas letter of 1984 says: "... It has been a rewarding year, because although we felt at the beginning of 1984, that we were just drifting along, by the end of the year, we are seeing signs of promise with new fellowship meetings starting; a telephone prayer chain, and a Church Family Weekend, planned for February."

It was a great joy to be part of the Church Family Weekend; Tom Hill, a youth worker for the District led the whole weekend, and it was a great success. Nearly 50 people boarded the coach for Weston-super-Mare in Somerset that Friday night, and those 50 knew and cared about each other in a much deeper way on the Sunday evening when we returned home.

As we prepared for the weekend away, we were given the sad news that Bob's sister, Mary, was terminally ill with cancer. She had not been too well when she attended Bob's father's funeral, and had steadily deteriorated, but didn't tell anyone. Bob had asked her, at the beginning of January, what the consultant had said to her, when she had visited him a day or two before; she replied that it was a nervous condition caused by the stress of Don's, her husband's, illness. This news was an awful shock to the whole family.

Round about the same time, we were asked to pray through the Telephone Prayer Chain for a little boy who was very ill with a rare form of cancer. Martin had been ill for a while, but his condition had worsened. The Telephone Prayer Chain consisted of a group of 12 people, who were committed to praying for the needs of others. A message was sent by telephone to each member; we all had one person to ring, and the final person in the Chain rang the first person; thus completing the chain. Immediately the message was received, as individuals, we prayed for the situation, and continued to pray regularly for about a month, when the request was reviewed. Every member was made very aware of the need for confidentiality; without that, the Prayer Chain would not have lasted 5 minutes; it continues to function, albeit in a different way. Bob found the Chain extremely useful and regularly gave us requests; we often found that when someone had used it once, they continued to come back; simply because it worked!

Within two or three weeks of our weekend away, Bob's sister died, in the hospital in Epsom, where she had been since we were given the news of her illness. We managed to get to see her a couple of times, the last time the day before she died. Her funeral took place in Epsom, in the April, a Memorial Service was held at Seahouses, Northumberland, [her home] at which Bob both led and preached.

As we arrived home from the funeral, that February day, we found my mother in a terrible state of shock. One of the members of the Ladies' Sisterhood, Connie Aris, had been found, battered to death, in her home that morning. Mum had taken the message on Bob's behalf, but it really upset her, and in fact, all the ladies of the Sisterhood, some of whom had been with her the previous afternoon at another meeting. It was at least six months before the funeral could take place, and police investigations went on long after that, but the murderer was never found. Connie lived only a few seconds walk from Cheltenham Spa railway station, and the police pointed out that it would have been very easy to get on a train and be miles away before anyone knew what had happened.

As winter changed into spring, little Martin's health began to deteriorate, and Bob popped in several times a week. Spring Bank Holiday Sunday found him very ill. Bob was told at the morning service, and spent a lot of the day with him at the family home; when he came home, he left himself just a couple of minutes to get ready for his evening service; as he arrived home I asked him how things were, his reply: "Absolutely awful', and he looked more upset than I had ever seen him before. I went with him to his preaching appointment at Shipton Oliffe, and right at the beginning of the service he led the congregation in prayer for Martin and his family. Martin died early on the Monday morning, a date I will never forget; 27th May, our fifteenth wedding anniversary.

After a very sad first half of the year, thankfully, the second half was very ordinary and routine; and it was with some relief that we reached the end.

Chapter Twenty Two

The Church Family Weekend of 1985 had been such a great success that another was planned for the end of January 1986; once more, it was led by Tom Hill and once more, it was a great success. Unfortunately, our euphoria was very short lived; within days, without warning, our Superintendent Minister left the Circuit, and we were all thrown into a state of bewilderment and shock. The Superintendent had always encouraged the ministers to talk over their problems in the Staff Meeting; they now realised that he had never shared his. Fortunately, Ernie Clarke had been appointed to the Circuit in 1983; he had been a Superintendent before, but wanted 'a quiet run down to retirement'; this was to be his last appointment. Ernie was able to step in, and take over the reins of the Circuit without any problem.

All the Circuit Staff lost their balance for a few weeks, but the minister who lived in Winchcombe was sheltered a little; Bob and Ernie, both living in the town, were thrown together to sort out many of the problems created by the sudden change in staffing. After two or three weeks we decided to get together just Dora and Ernie, and Bob and I. Ernie treated us all to a meal at the local Berni Inn one lunch time and it began a trend that lasted until Bob's death. Every two or three months we would get together for a meal, the one who was paying chose the venue, but in reality, we almost always ended up in the Pizza Hut in Cheltenham! Once Dora and Ernie retired in 1989, we would go to them for a meal at their new home in Dursley, Gloucestershire, only about 30-45 minutes away from Cheltenham, and they would come to us - often still at the Pizza Hut. Once we moved from Cheltenham we continued to meet, this time in Taunton, half way between Dursley and Launceston; when Bob was too ill to travel, Dora and Ernie came to us.

In 1988, there was great excitement within Methodism, as we celebrated the 250th Anniversary of the Conversion of John and Charles Wesley; Bob was one of the Wesleys' greatest admirers, and threw himself into the celebrations with great vigour. The highlight was a magnificent service in Gloucester Cathedral, which both moved and impressed all who were present.

But St Mark's people were also caught up in a celebration of a different kind, when our Girls' Brigade Captain, Ann Blenkinsopp, married one of our Church Stewards, Stephen Varley, on 16th April. Both had grown up in the church, and had not taken much notice of each other, but had joined a working party to paint the inside of the Shipton Oliffe Chapel; people began to watch the relationship blossom from that moment on.

Ann's mother had come originally from Halifax, and Bob had discovered very early in our ministry in Cheltenham, that Ann's grandfather had been one of his members in the Halifax Wesley Circuit. He made great play of this in the wedding address:

> Little did I know when I left Headingley in 1965 to go to my first appointment as a Methodist minister in Halifax, that I would have as one of my members, a gentleman who is here today. When I first met Harry Huntsman, I didn't know he had a grand-daughter by the name of Ann, and that one day I would marry her - or at least, conduct the Marriage Service.

> And little did I know in those days, that just over the hill from Halifax, is Bradford, and from the Lidgett Green area of that city, a young woman by the name of Mary, would later marry another Yorkshire tike from Menston, near Guisley, and close to the world famous 'Harry Ramsden's Fish and Chip Restaurant'. And that later still, they would produce a Norfolk Dumpling they'd call Stephen.

> I must congratulate you Stephen, for three things. First of all, the choice of a wife who can cook (Ann's profession), and that's no reflection on my wife's ability in that field. I love the story of the couple, and their first morning in their own home after the honeymoon. The young husband was a bit like me - he got up, went downstairs to the kitchen, and some time later took breakfast up to his bride. "There", he said, "What do you think of that?" She gazed at the tea, the bacon and eggs, the toast, marmalade, all nicely set out on the tray, and she said, "Why, that's wonderful."

> "Yes", said her husband, "And that's how I want breakfast every morning". So Stephen, congratulations on making sure that your wife can cook.

> Secondly, I have to congratulate you on your choice of Best Man. I know you have two brothers, and I know too, that both Martin and Robert would have coped well in that capacity; but what

wisdom in selecting a fellow Geordie to act as your Best Man, a fellow Geordie from South Shields. 'You yems in Sooth Shiels. Am from Beddleton - 12 miles north of New Cassel'. English translation: I believe your home was in South Shields; I'm from the town of Bedlington, some 12 miles north of Newcastle'. Stephen, it's just amazing that we have similar taste, and we know quality when we see it.

And then, thirdly, Stephen - but this does include Ann as well; I must congratulate you both on the enormous amount of thought and prayer, which has gone into the preparations for this Marriage Service,(at this point Bob produced a print-out - his instructions from the Bride and Groom!) The choice of hymns, with the first tune 'Dying Stephen', and the final hymn, with the Gloucestershire connection in the tune 'Thornbury', a place that is dear to the Blenkinsopps - Ann's grandparents live there! But the hymn sandwich contains many goodies and much nourishment.

For one thing, the way in which Stephen and Ann have so ordered the arrangements, means that I can't now switch to automatic pilot. I have to think carefully, and stick to the brief given by the bride and groom. It's so refreshing to have readings other than the great words of St Paul in 1 Corinthians 13. Your choice of Colossians 3 is right, not least because it's one of my favourite readings: 'Put on love, which binds everything together in perfect harmony. And let the peace of Christ rule in your hearts and be thankful.' And what about that short passage from the Gospel, where Jesus talked about man and woman becoming one.

As you've both had experience of working with children and young people, you might appreciate this story of the Sunday School teacher, showing pictures to her class, and asking them to quote some verse from the Bible which the picture suggested. The first picture was of two children, with arms around each other. A boy put his hand up and offered the verse: 'Love one another'. 'Very good' said the teacher.

Another picture was of a little girl, listening very attentively to her mother. Another child offered the verse of scripture 'Obey your parent'.

Then a third picture was held up, showing two boys pulling on the opposite ends of the same cat. The children were nonplussed – hadn't a clue, until one child piped up: 'What God hath joined together, let no man put asunder'.

Going back to that reading in Colossians 3 – There's a certain member of the choir, who shall remain nameless, who insists that, whenever I read that passage, I read verse 18 as well. We usually stop at the words 'Whatever you do, in word or deed, do everything in the name of the Lord Jesus, giving thanks to God, the Father, through Him'. Verse 18, for those who may be interested, reads: 'Wives submit to your husbands', and all the men in the congregation respond heartily with the Amens!

It's never easy to pinpoint the moment when a friendship between two people develops into a romance, and leads, eventually, to an occasion like this. But sticking my neck out, I would suggest that a certain working party, set up to re-decorate the Methodist Chapel at Shipton Oliffe had something to do with it. Ann and Stephen spent hours and hours together making the little chapel beautiful. Stephen does help on the rota of organists who play on Sunday evenings; and many of you know that the organ there is still pumped by hand. Faithful Albert Hambling, very experienced from many years of practice, plays an essential part in enabling the organist to function properly.

There is a lovely story of a village church, like Shipton, where the organist decided to put on a recital. After each item on the programme, the organist would stand up, bow to the audience, and then announce his next piece, usually saying 'For my next piece…' This went on through the recital until the poor organ-blower, who, by this time was sweating at the gills, and getting rather annoyed, could stand it no longer. After a certain piece the organist stood up, as usual, to announce his next piece, sat down and began to run his fingers over the keyboard, but not a sound was heard. He stood to announce the number again: 'for my next piece…' and still there was no sound. Then the head of the organ blower appeared from behind the curtain, and he said to the organist 'Not so much of 'For my next piece', let's have a little more we, in it!'

There's a lesson for any couple starting out, as Ann and Stephen are doing; or for some of us well along the road. Make this service an opportunity for you to renew your marriage vows.

We rejoice with you both today, and pray God's blessing upon your marriage, and we pledge our continued support. Let me close with a couple of short, humorous stories. Later in the service Stephen and Ann will make vows to each other and there are familiar words used at that point.

Two little girls were heard talking together just after a wedding ceremony. The first girl said: 'How many wives did the Minister say that men could have?' The second girl answered: 'Why one of course!' 'That's funny' said the first little girl, 'I was sure I heard him say 16: four better, four worse, four richer, four poorer, you see, 16'.

Well, Stephen, I expect one is enough. But quite seriously, being a husband is like any other job. It helps a lot if you like the boss!

In September of 1988, we went over to see Bob's brother-in-law, Don, when he was staying with his daughter, Gill. Don had remarried, and he and his American wife, Ginny, were living happily in the northern part of New York State; they were over in England for Ginny's first visit, and we wanted to take the opportunity to see them. Bob only had a morning preaching appointment on 25th September due to all the Harvest weekends, with the pulpits filled by guest preachers. We had a lovely time with them, and got back home at about 9 p.m.

Soon after we arrived home, we had a 'phone call from John telling us that he was a Dad; Charlotte Amy, our first grandchild had been born that afternoon, and all was well.

Bob adored his first grandchild, and took many photos of her, as did our friend, Bob Richards, a farmer and a photographer, who had over the years taken many photos of each member of the family.

David, Bob, Paul and John in Cheltenham.

With George Thomas, Mr Speaker, in the Speaker's home in the Houses of Parliament. July 1981.

Christmas lunch. Every year, we had to make hats from one sheet of wrapping paper and three sewing pins! The picture shows Sarah, John, Paul and Bob's Mum wearing their hats.

Christmas in Cheltenham. Back row, from the left: Bob, Joy, Rachael, David, Therese [Paul's wife], Paul, Sarah. Sitting in the front. Joy's Mum [on the left] and Bob's Mum.

The last family photo – August 1992. With all the children, their spouses, and Bob's first four granddaughters, Charlotte, Samantha, Katarina and Georgia.

Bob, Rachael, Sarah, Joy, and Joy's Mum.

Chapter Twenty Three

As I have said before, Bob had a wonderful sense of humour, and it was really in Cheltenham that it came to the fore. I think this was for several reasons. Our marriage was very strong, and the difficulties that we had experienced in the early years had all gone; also, he was very happy in his ministry there. He had overcome the self-doubts that had been a problem in previous appointments, and he knew he was deeply loved by the churches over which he had pastoral charge. It was during this time that he found his particular niche within the Methodist Ministry, and he was very happy. The result was a sense of humour that his church members loved, and many practical jokes which were played at the expense of the family. To omit these would detract from the person that Bob was, and yet to include them in some of the more serious parts of his story would be unseemly, so I have decided to give them a chapter all to themselves!

These days, I only have to see one of those round, red vacuum cleaners, with a handle on the top, to be reminded of the day that Bob buckled two belts together, looped them through the vacuum cleaner handle, and put the belts diagonally across his shoulder, with the cleaner hanging at his side, and the hose, with the brush on the end, in his hand, coming down the stairs singing the theme tune from the film 'Ghostbusters'.

Or to watch the Remembrance service from the Royal Albert Hall, and see the Chelsea Pensioners marking time before they process down the stairs and into the places reserved for them, to remember our stairs in Cheltenham. Being a Victorian house, the staircase was quite wide, and if either of the girls or myself happen to be coming down the stairs at the same time as Bob, then we were made to link arms with him, and mark time, before walking down the stairs together, as Bob sang the song that is always played for the Pensioners on that occasion.

Sarah remembers, very clearly, the morning, one weekend, when she was called to get up, and wandered, half-asleep, to the bathroom. She slid her hand between the shower curtain and the wall in order to switch the shower on, only to have her hand grabbed; she screamed the house down! Bob was standing, fully clothed, in the shower, intending to make her jump, but when he saw her hand appear, and realised that the shower was about to be turned on, he knew that he would get wet, and grabbed her hand to stop her. When I challenged him as to what he thought he was doing, he said: "Well, I was going to get wet!" My response? "But what were you doing there in the first place?"

You could never say to Bob, 'don't do that', because he was likely to take it as a challenge. One evening, we were going to a concert at Sarah's school, in which the school orchestra was playing in the second half; Sarah was playing the clarinet. Her last words to her dad were: "Don't wave at me". Bob's response was to find a seat in the back row; as soon as the orchestra took their seats, he stood up and waved at Sarah. She tried to ignore him, but the girl next to her commented: "Look at that daft man waving". Sarah responded with the comment: "What a twit." She never acknowledged that he was her father!

One afternoon, after school, Rachael was in the bathroom; when Bob realised this, he rushed up the stairs, and pleaded with her to come out. Rachael was quite adamant that she would come out when she was done, but Bob, by now standing outside the door, continued to plead with her to come out immediately. Eventually she came out, and Bob rushed in - to take cling film off the top of the china part of the toilet, put there as a joke for Sarah, but knowing that Rachael wouldn't appreciate it at all.

Another occasion found him making the morning drink; he prepared tea for himself and me, and coffee for my mother. As she was drinking her coffee, he asked Mum several times if her coffee was all right - to the extent that she asked him what he had done to it. It turned out that he had run out of hot water in the kettle, and rather than boil more, he topped her coffee up with tea from the teapot.

But the one thing that really sticks in my mind, is a practical joke that altered over quite a long period of time.

This began one night when Bob got out of bed and paid a visit to the toilet; having been disturbed, I decided to pop along to the toilet when he came back. As I returned to the bedroom, I wandered, half asleep, through the door, and got the shock of my life, when Bob jumped out from behind the door. I forgot all about this, until several weeks later, he did the same again. After this, I was on my guard, and used to look through the crack in the door, in order to find out where he was before I walked into the room.

The prank continued and evolved from hiding behind the door, to lying on the floor at the far side of the bed, and so on, until the final time, when I found him trying to stand on an exercise bike, which he had moved from the corner where it normally stood, to the front of the wardrobe. When I asked him what he was doing, he said: "Well, I thought that if I could just get on top of the wardrobe, you'd never find me up there!"

These few stories, I hope, give you just a flavour of life with Bob, which was never dull, and the family take great delight in reliving these wonderful memories, which make us laugh over and over again.

Chapter Twenty Four

In January, February and March 1989 Bob took a Sabbatical. He had decided to look at spirituality in the light of various religious orders; as a result he spent almost two weeks in Prinknash Abbey, near Cheltenham, a Benedictine order; one week at Hilfield Friary, a Franciscan order in Dorset, and several days in an ecumenical order, nearing the end of its life, near Guildford, Surrey. He far preferred his time at Hilfield, and that too, changed him spiritually.

At the beginning of March it was a real joy to share with David and Olga in their Greek Orthodox wedding in London. It was a new and wonderful experience for us, which broadened the horizon of our faith, and the music was wonderful. This joy was deepened, as a year later, we shared with them again, this time in the Greek Orthodox christening of their first child Katarina.

We arrived in Cheltenham in 1979; Rev Tom Meadley and his wife Joan were already settled in retirement there. Tom had been Bob's Principal at Cliff College in 1960, and Bob loved, admired and respected him greatly. Although we didn't meet up together that often, Bob always valued the time he spent with Tom. In the spring of 1989 Tom had a stroke, and died on 25th May, 1989; Bob had tried to visit him every day during his last illness, and this stirred within him a longing to go back to Cliff College for the Celebration Weekend.

Bob was the only member of the family who had ever been and we were all keen to go to see what the place was like. We went on Spring Bank Holiday Monday, 1989, just a few days after Tom's death. It was a life-changing experience for all of us.

For Bob, it was a very different Celebration to the ones he had experienced nearly thirty years before; but it was the final step in his journey that took him back to his spiritual roots. He had an evangelical conversion, but had slowly lost a lot of his evangelical fervour; that Monday took him back into the Saviour's arms, and into a deeper relationship with Jesus; a relationship that grew and deepened daily, and that was to be his strength and comfort in the difficult times ahead.

For me, it deepened my love for Jesus, and led me into a closer relationship with Him, a growing relationship that has never stopped since that day.

For the girls it was an experience they had never known in quite the same way before, and they relished every moment of it. For Rachael, it was a further confirmation of her commitment to Jesus, and for Sarah, it was a real joy to be with other young people as they worshipped in a way that was very different to the way she worshipped in the local church.

We got home that night, and sang, accompanied by Rachael on the piano, all the songs we had learned that day – and more!

Rachael had decided that she liked the idea of being a student at Cliff, and was thinking about applying for the course; this would mean her taking a year out before going to University, something she was already planning to do. A day or two after the "Cliff Experience" she told us "I would like to go, but before I make a final decision, I would like to talk to someone who has been a student there recently." We should not be surprised that God provided her with two ex-students!

The following Sunday, Andy and Bev Lyle walked into our lives. They had both been students at Cliff – that is where they met! They were now working for Langley House Trust; a Christian charity, whose mission is "to work with those who are at risk of offending, or have offended, establishing positive foundations so that they can lead crime-free lives and become contributors to society". Having worked for a while at Wing Grange, they had just been sent to work at The Knole, in Cheltenham. It was not long before Rachael had decided – she applied to Cliff and was accepted as a student for the year 1990-91 – exactly thirty years after her Dad was there!

Through Andy and Bev's work with the Mission Band at St Mark's, several young people made a commitment to Jesus, and are all still active Christians today. Within the first three weeks of the Mission Band being formed, the baby that Bev was expecting was born; we were all devastated to learn that the baby, Hannah, was very poorly. The Mission Band decided to meet for prayer in the only place available – Sarah's bedroom! It was transformed from a tip into a suitable place for a prayer meeting, in record time. Little Hannah Ruth lived only three days, but her short life has become a bond between our two families, and one that will never go away.

As the year progressed, Rachael set out to raise money to pay her fees for Cliff, and was very well supported by the Church and Circuit. Many fundraising events took place, and the excitement and sense of anticipation grew, month by month, until the time for her departure grew near.

Chapter Twenty Five

1990 saw all the preliminaries taking place as we thought about leaving Cheltenham. We had decided to leave in the summer of 1991 after twelve very happy years; the last two of which Bob was the Superintendent Minister, having taken over when Ernie Clarke retired. At Ernie and Dora's farewell, Bob was 'hailed' as the new 'Super', and in a mock ceremony, Ernie, very solemnly presented him with his 'badge of office' in the form of the "Circuit Cycle Clips"!!

Once the decision was made that we would leave, we had to prepare a fifty word statement about ourselves and the sort of appointment we were looking for. This is much harder than it sounds, and we knew that this 'perfect' situation that we envisaged for ourselves, just didn't exist, so we were prepared to compromise.

We had made up our minds that, although one of the new rules that came into being that year, enabled us to approach up to five Circuits at a time about an appointment, we would rather leave the Circuits to approach us; we felt we would find it easier to discern God's will that way.

We were approached, first of all by the Launceston Circuit, and took this up by a visit to look at the chapels and to meet the Circuit officials. I well remember a wonderful meal at the Senior Circuit Steward's home: Graham and Catherine Jones lived in a lovely farmhouse, just a couple of miles outside Launceston – Graham was a sheep farmer among other things. The meal had been prepared by all the Circuit Stewards' wives, and Margaret Baker had made a beautiful raspberry pavlova; Bob loved meringue, and after his second helping, said to Margaret: "If you'll make me one of these every week, I'll come!!" I have learned since, that when Les Baker asked Bob about his accomplishments, his reply was: "I won the snooker cup at college!"

Although we had other offers, we felt that Launceston was the right place to be, and accepted the invitation; we only had to complain about one thing – Launceston is about one hour's drive further from Cheltenham than we had hoped!!

Also in June, we had the excitement of the birth of another grandchild. Frances and John were eagerly awaiting the birth of a brother or sister for Charlotte, and so were we! On 27th June, Samantha Emily arrived, and we were all thrilled. We dashed up to see her when she was just a few days old, with a mop of hair, just like her big sister.

After all the excitement, we settled down for our final year in Gloucestershire. We had a lovely break during the summer, as we visited our friends Jan and David Girt and their family in Gateshead. David was a Church Army Captain, and we got to know them both long before they were married, when we all were living in Watford. 1990 was an important year for Gateshead because the Garden Festival was taking place that summer, and we were able to spend a glorious day there; it was exhausting, but well worth the visit. We persuaded my mother to use a wheelchair, as the walking would have been too much for her, but Bob found it very frustrating - every time we got in a crowd, she offered to get out and walk, at the top of her voice!! After a happy week there, we moved on to Sheffield.

Rosemary and Tony Fawthrop had been Sunday School teachers and Youth Leaders in my home church at South Harrow, and had known me since I was twelve. They moved to Sheffield with Tony's work, and we had called on them once or twice, but never stayed with them. Now they had asked us to stay because they were close to Cliff – I should say that they had invited us lots of times, but it had not been possible before. We thought it would be good to see the Peak District, and to get the feel of the area where Rachael would be spending the next year; so we stayed from the Saturday until the Wednesday morning.

On the Monday, we went to Bakewell. We had been told it was Market Day and a good day to go; so straight after breakfast, we set off. Bakewell is the home of the famous tart, although its correct title, we were told, is Bakewell Pudding. On arrival, we went into a local hotel for a cup of coffee and a slice of home-made Bakewell pudding. We took our time, and when we were ready to leave, Grandma, Sarah and I all decided to visit the ladies toilet before we went any further; Rachael and Bob waited for us outside. As we emerged Bob greeted us with the words: "Why are you always in the toilet when something exciting happens?" It turned out that a young bullock had escaped from the Market and ran down the street to the hotel, Bob jumped in front of it to deflect it from going into the town, and it ran into the entrance hall of the hotel; by the time all this had happened, the farmer had caught up with it and led it back to the Market. We all had a good laugh, and later, Bob proudly showed everyone the photos he took of the proceedings; he named them 'The Bullfighter'!

From Bakewell, we took a leisurely drive to Chatsworth Park, where we found a picnic area, and decided it was time to eat our lunch. We parked in a spot that suited everyone – not an easy task when you have five very different people in the vehicle! We had only just got settled when a huge swarm of tiny flies surrounded the car; it became obvious that it would be impossible to eat with the window open, let alone sit outside the car, so Bob moved the car to a different spot; two minutes later the flies arrived! This happened several times, and in the end, we parked right on the edge of the parking area, quite a distance from where we started! At last we had peace, and began to eat, but as we looked across the picnic area we saw some people, who had, minutes before, been enjoying their lunch, start fly-swatting, and eventually cleared their picnic away and got back in their car, we had obviously passed the flies on to them!

As we were eating our lunch, Bob complained of a pain in his groin, and we both thought he had pulled a muscle, or given himself a hernia, when he jumped in front of the bullock. We didn't realise at the time, but this was the first symptom of his final illness.

The rest of our time was very enjoyable, and we had a lovely day out with Rosemary, Tony and Rosemary's mum; the two 'Grans' got on well together, they were the same age and both came from the suburbs of North London, and what's more, they both enjoyed knitting, embroidery etc.

When we arrived home at the beginning of August, we were greeted by Rebecca Reed. Rebecca is the daughter of our good friends Matney and Mildred Reed, from Tennessee; having spent many years teaching, she had returned to college – Vanderbilt in Nashville, and studied for the United Methodist Ministry. In the summer of 1990, she was due to have some practical experience, working alongside an experienced minister; Rebecca asked permission to work with Bob. She arrived in the middle of June for ten weeks; her studies were supervised by Rev Terry Spencer, one of our colleagues, who had pastoral charge of the churches at Winchcombe and Bishop's Cleeve, so we felt free to go away for ten days, added to which, we felt she might like a breathing space from the family; life in our chaotic household was not everyone's cup of tea.

The summer was over all too soon; Rebecca left at the end of August, and within two weeks, Rachael left to begin her year at Cliff College.

On 15th September, 1990 we set off to take Rachael to Cliff, and once she was settled in her room, we paid her a very tearful farewell, and made our way back to Cheltenham – I must have cried for the first half hour of the journey!

Bob was so proud of the fact that Rachael was at Cliff; he was forever grateful for all the college had done for him, and the knowledge that his daughter would also go through the "Cliff Experience" thrilled him to bits.

Chapter Twenty Six

As the autumn progressed, Bob felt more 'under the weather'; he had gone straight to the doctor on our return from holiday, and after many visits, he was referred to Cheltenham General Hospital. In the late autumn, he was tested for kidney stones, and although the X-ray showed none, his symptoms so closely resembled them that the conclusion was drawn that he had a translucent stone which did not show up on the X-rays. On 27th December he was seen by the consultant, and he was admitted for treatment on 21st February.

During all this time he kept working, but he spent every available moment lying on the settee. As time went on, it became more and more obvious to all who knew him that he was far from well. As I look back now I am amazed at the determination which kept him going, and especially so, when I remember that only a day or so before he was due to go to hospital, he drove us all to Ruislip, near London, to take the funeral of my mother's dear friend, our next door neighbour from my childhood, Emily Watson.

The operation took place the next day, but instead of the expected kidney stone, the surgeon found a blockage; a biopsy was taken, and Bob had to wait for a week for the result.

For some reason, whenever Bob was in hospital, he kept, in a notebook, a detailed account of his visitors; the events of the day; and his own thoughts and feelings.

On Monday, 25th February he recorded
Devotions – read Hebrews 11: 8-12, 17-19, 2 Corinthians 4: 1-8 – dwelt on verses 16-18: 'though our outward nature is wasting away; our inner nature is being renewed every day'... Also 'Cast the burden of the present, along with the sin of the past and the fear of the future, upon the Lord.'

Tuesday 26th February:
For meditation, quoted from memory MHB 60: HP 64 (he meant 62!) – 'Captain of Israel's host'.

Also: - 'Ah! Show me that happiest place,
The place of Thy people's abode.
Where saints in an ecstasy gaze,
And hang on a crucified God.
Thy love for a sinner declare,
Thy passion and death on the tree.
My Spirit to Calvary bear, and suffer
and triumph with Thee' CW

Thought much about, our lovely family; of Joy, a devoted partner for nearly 21 years, and stepmother to Paul, John and David. The struggles through those adolescent years. The joy of seeing the boys settled; Paul and Therese happily married and pursuing careers in the medical field. At present, Therese, Sister in Casualty at Birmingham General; Paul, a Registrar in the Lancaster Royal Infirmary, and both off to Omaha, Nebraska, in July.

John, Frances, Charlotte and Samantha; lovely to 'call in on' Feb. 20th on the way back from Auntie Watson's funeral. What a change in Samantha.

David, Olga and Katarina, who is a dear.

How thankful that Joy and I decided to have our own family, what a blessing to have Rachael and Sarah – so different, but both precious. Rachael thoroughly enjoying her 'year out' at Cliff College, prior to University. Finding a great satisfaction in Preaching, and by August, will have completed her Local Preacher's studies.

Sarah – approaching G.C.S.E. Finals in May/June. Fully involved in Church life: Choir; G.B. [Girl's Brigade]; SMOG [St Mark's Other Group - Youth Group!]; Mission Band, and looking forward to preaching the sermon on April 7th. Also mentally prepared to move, in August, to Launceston. What blessings we've received in our married life.

Tuesday P.M. Devotions:

Matt: 6: 24-34
v 25 'Do not be anxious about your life...'

v 34 'Do not be anxious about tomorrow...'
Meditate on these words, and rest, confident in the Lord's promise.

Philippians 4: v6
'Have no anxiety about anything, but in everything, by prayer and supplication, with thanksgiving, let your requests be made known to God, and the peace of God, which passes all understanding, will keep your hearts and your minds in Christ Jesus... whatever is lovely, whatever is gracious... think on these things... not that I complain of want, for I have learned, in whatever state I am, to be content...I can do all things, through Christ who strengthens me.'

Saturday March 2nd 1991

8.30 a.m. Mr KINDER (the Consultant)
A growth in the bladder pressing on tube and restricting the flow. The difficulties of passing water, probably due to disturbance when he carried out the internal investigation, and the sample of tissue. Take out catheter Monday - it should probably start flowing on its own.

They will continue to gather information, including a scan, and decide on the best course of treatment – will probably mean surgery. He will come and discuss whatever he feels is best, with me, in due course.

Saturday, March 2nd (contd.)

The day when Mr Kinder broke the news about the growth in the bladder. The worst news I've ever received, and throughout the day my mind has dwelt on it. Is it malignant or benign? That will be determined when further tests are carried out.

Rang Joy with the news at 11 a.m. Felt she ought to know, before this afternoon's visiting. The Lord will bless and keep her.

She seemed quite composed when she came, but I was glad she rang and spoke to Paul. It will be good to see him and Therese tomorrow.

Sister Dean came into the Day Room to chat about the news. It was good to have her share. Watched Columbo, but didn't really get into it.

After the News, jotting down my thoughts before turning to Devotions. Ps.46; Ps 139; Matt. 6: 24-34; Philippians 4: 2; Cor. 12: 1-10. Will remember Joy and the family before I turn to sleep.

March 3rd JOY'S BIRTHDAY

Slept reasonably well until 3.30 a.m. and then tossed and turned – all kinds of thoughts filling the mind.

Bathroom at 5.55 a.m; remember quoting a verse from the Sermon on the Mount and Psalm 118.

'Take no thought for tomorrow' and 'This is the day which the Lord hath made, let us rejoice and be glad in it.'

Tuesday, March 5th ...

Mr Verma came to tell me the change of procedure. Cancer of the prostate, not a growth in the bladder. Bone scan to be organised. Start me on some hormone treatment, Radiotherapy and Chemotherapy (not the drastic kind).

From this point on, Bob's hospital diary recorded visitors and reminders of things that needed to be done in the Circuit. He left hospital on 14th March, and was eventually back at work at the beginning of June, feeling very fit. During his time in hospital, he had repeatedly told me that all he wanted to do was to preach again; he wasn't concerned about the rest of the work, but he couldn't imagine life without preaching.

Chapter Twenty Seven

Bob was no sooner back at work, than it was time to prepare for our move to Launceston, and we were very grateful for the help that many of our friends gave us, as we began to pack.

Our final services at St Mark's were the last Sunday of July; in the morning, I led the worship and Bob preached, in the evening, we reversed our roles.

It was our joy to go to Cliff on Sunday, 5th August, for the "End of Year" service. After the certificates were presented to the students, an invitation was given to anyone who felt they had something to say; Bob waited until they were about to move on to the next stage of the service, and then rushed out. He talked about all that Cliff had done for him thirty years before, having changed him, in a year, from a rough coal miner, to a man ready to follow a call into the ministry. He wanted to record, in front of the 1990/91 year students, his grateful thanks at being given the opportunity and privilege to spend a year there.

Once Rachael was home, we worked hard for the final two weeks before we moved. Our home had a large cellar, and we were embarrassed that we had accumulated so much rubbish over twelve years, that we needed a large builder's skip to clear it all away!

Many people in Cheltenham have fond memories of Bob. Megan Harvey wrote:
> When I was ill twelve/thirteen years ago, Bob did so much to help … when I came back from the (operating) theatre to Intensive Care … there he was. I thought: I'm O.K. if Bob is here. He was one of my most regular visitors.
>
> Then four months later, when I had a second op., he was there again … I couldn't cope with anyone, except Bob, and he would sit and talk and had such a calming effect; It was wonderful … he was a gentle man, but with a lovely sense of humour … I remember, when we had not been for several weeks, I said 'Sorry we haven't been for so long, Bob', and he said 'Don't worry, as long as you send the money, that's all we want!!!!'
> And again, one Sunday, it started to rain when we came out:

That's your fault, Megan. We haven't had rain for weeks!!!

He was a tonic, and the world is a poorer place without him.

Ada and Ron Fletcher remember the last time they saw Bob, when they visited him in Launceston:

One outstanding memory we have, was when we last saw Bob in his wheelchair. He had a painful spasm, but when he came through from his bedroom, he was singing. That is something we will never forget ... His body may have changed in appearance, but the 'old Bob' was still evident.

Ann Humphris wrote
On his very last evening service at St Mark's on the way out, he shook my husband's hand and said 'Nice to see you, Garry.' Now Garry had been to St Mark's maybe a dozen times whilst Bob was there. How did he remember Garry's name? I was so touched – but then that was Bob. I know Garry was always impressed with Bob – and he wanted to be at Bob's last service – in the same way that he wanted to attend his Thanksgiving Service, and willingly drove Nic and me down to Launceston. Our girls, Sally and Nic always spoke so well of Bob, and we were always so thrilled that he could officiate at Sally and Charles' wedding – we have a wonderful video of Bob at work, on that occasion!

A friend, whom we first met when she taught Rachael and Sarah at Primary School, Jean Ford wrote:
Bob was one of the nicest people I have ever met, and his death has made the world a poorer place.

A member of St Mark's, Ruth Slade says:
...remembrances of Bob bring thoughts of his feelings for people; his understanding of situations, the young and the elderly. Everyone had a warm welcome into the family ... Bob always made his preaching interesting and different. I'll always remember an Ash Wednesday Service ... it was a very heart-searching time, and really brought home the personal meaning of repentance. I feel Bob was a man, a minister, who brought the love of Christ to us all, without inhibition, and so easy to approach.

George Kirkham was at St Mark's for the last few years of our time there:

I came to St Mark's Church in October 1987 – not a very happy man, still grieving the loss of my dear wife. I made myself known to Bob, and the warmth of his greeting made me feel at once, that I could settle in the church, and know I had a friend that would care about me. Soon afterwards, I met Joy and the girls, and knew there was a happy, Christian family, that was Bob's background.

It was soon obvious that Bob's background, as a coal miner, had given him an understanding of the needs of ordinary men and women. He knew how to laugh, often when joking against himself, and his love for children and young folk in church was apparent.

His kindness and concern for folk in hospital was appreciated by me when I had my knee operation, and for several other folk I know who were not Methodists. His passing left the world and Methodism with a sad loss.

Vera Fowler was not a member of any church in our section, but was a member at Whaddon, on the other side of the town.

I first came to Cheltenham in 1981, and joined the Whaddon Church as it was my nearest Methodist Church. I guess it was about 5-6 weeks after I joined that Bob came to take our morning service. I was still feeling, at that time, rather an outsider, and missed Hendon Church and my friends very much.

After the service, Bob shook hands and asked if I was visiting. I told him I had moved to Prestbury a few weeks previously, and he asked where I came from; I told him Hendon in London. He immediately knew who our minister was, saying that our minister was Rev Ramsey Moor, who he knew because he had been in Watford, the same District; he said he thought he had seen me before, and we agreed it may have been at District Synod, which I had attended. I shall never forget that conversation, and his friendliness, when I was feeling quite alone. It made me realise that it was this great Methodist Family that mattered, wherever I was, and that I belonged. From then, I never really looked back.

From St Mark's, Rhoda and Guy Norton and Rhoda's mother, Vera Harper, wrote:

Bob was a charismatic man, who always made you feel better for seeing him. If a patient in hospital, you would feel an uplift of spirit. His acknowledgement at a church 'do', if only a wink, made you feel part of the Church family. I liked the way he would introduce his family into the sermon ... it was an advantage to Bob, to have lived in the world, as it were, before joining the ministry.

Since we left Cheltenham, both Joan and 'Mac' McDonald have passed away, but after Bob and Joan's deaths, Mac wrote to tell me of two occasions that had remained in his memory.

1) In earlier days, when Joan had a very major operation, Bob was the first to bring comforting news of the outcome. At a later date, for a second op he was there again, to bring the happy result to a fretful husband.

2) You may well recall Bob's Sabbatical. We were aimlessly driving around Cranham Woods (not thinking then of Bob), and decided to nose down into Prinknash. The car park, as expected, was empty, except for a group of workers, in overalls, slaving away at a huge bonfire. One of the group lugging a large tree cutting, dropped same and approached us. Feeling like trespassers, we were 'tickled pink' to have found our lost minister – Bob Wilson we presume!!

From Rev Norman Brookes in New Zealand, who served for a year in Cheltenham before our arrival, but spent some time with us just weeks before our move to Launceston:

As you know, we did not have a great deal of face to face contact with Bob, though we met when he visited the Circuit in 1977 (I think) (actually it was February 1978), prior to taking up the Cheltenham appointment. Then, of course, we met again, two years ago when Bob kindly invited me to preach at St Mark's. I have fond memories of meeting both Bob and yourself prior to that service, and then of the way in which Bob led the service, questioning us about the church in New Zealand etc.

But we have been blessed by Bob's ministry in other ways, even in New Zealand – especially by reading the many thoughtful letters from the Minister that he wrote in St Mark's Messenger (Church Magazine) which we still receive.

Bob was a person I would have enjoyed working with. His faith and love were deeply appreciated by many in Cheltenham. May God give you strength for today and tomorrow.

Finally, some thoughts from Joy Wills. Joy was for many years a Church Steward at Bishops Cleeve (not part of our section), and also, the wife of Bill Wills, the Circuit Steward, who first approached us from the Cheltenham Circuit, early in 1978.

I have been thinking about Bob's work, here in the Circuit; he was always so approachable, kind and thoughtful, gave so much of himself in all he did. He was always early for services and meetings, as a Steward, this was much appreciated.

When he must have been in constant pain, he patiently waited for his hospital appointment, and amidst many difficulties, carried on with his work – a wonderful example to us all. He always had time for people, no matter how many other things needed his attention …

It was a privilege to have been allowed to stay so long in Cheltenham, and we all knew it, but we also knew that we would have to move on some time; we felt that that time had come, and that God was calling us to Launceston, and so we prepared ourselves for 'pastures new.'
But the time spent in Cheltenham was very special. We were fortunate to have had many Christmases with the whole family around us; Paul and Therese came as their hospital shifts allowed; John always came, initially on his own, but later with his current girlfriend; and David came as his shifts in the catering trade allowed. By the time we moved, all the boys were in settled relationships, and starting their own families, but we never again had Christmases in the way we had during those years, and they are still greatly missed.

Chapter Twenty Eight

We moved out of Gloucester Road on 19th August, 1991; it was an emotional wrench after twelve years, but the excitement of a new home, a new town, and a new Circuit, took over from the sadness of so many goodbyes.

We arrived in Launceston at about 8.30 p.m.; and were welcomed at the Manse in Hendra Gardens, with a cup of tea and the familiar faces of Brian and Glennis Tunbridge, the Circuit Treasurer and his wife. We had planned to sleep in the empty house, but were delighted to have been provided with sunbeds (for Bob and I) to sleep on; the girls were happy on the floor!

Mum was to stay with another Circuit Steward – Les Baker and his wife, Margaret; and it was about 9 p.m. when we arrived there for an evening meal. We had a lovely time with them, and they have always been very supportive of all the family.

Sleep that night was not as bad as we had anticipated; but we were thankful to have time to get ourselves organised, as the removal van was later arriving than originally planned.

Our friends, Mary and Peter Jones, from Cheltenham, had planned their holiday to coincide with our move; they were staying in Bude and arrived to help us unpack; once the removal van had gone Margaret and Les Baker helped us too; not only in emptying boxes of china etc., but also providing us with hot meals – it was wonderful to be surrounded by such caring people.

Our official welcome to the circuit was two weeks later, at the beginning of September, and our friends, Kath and Keith Bass, from Watford, joined us for that occasion. The service was all that we had hoped it would be, and it was good to meet many of the people amongst whom we would be working for the foreseeable future.

It was lovely to have Rachael home again, but all too soon it was time for her to start University in Lancaster. We shared the driving on the outward journey, but once we had settled Rachael in her room, Bob drove all the way home; he was absolutely worn out, but he managed to summon up the energy to go to the Harvest Supper at our second largest church – Pipers Pool.

Our section of the Circuit consisted of Central, a large church of about 300 members in the centre of Launceston; Pipers Pool, five miles out from the town, with several active young families involved there; and three small chapels, also several miles from the town: Kennards House, Tregada and Lewannick Chapel; the latter had closed not long before we arrived, but the Methodists continued to worship in the village hall.

After Bob's first service at Pipers Pool, a lunch was held, so that we could get to know the members; it was a lovely day, and the meal was served outside, on a patch of grass near the cemetery! Bob commented that it was the first time he had had a sit down meal in a grave yard!!

As we moved into autumn, our lives settled down and it was good to start to feel that we belonged. The highlights of that first autumn stand out in my memory: the meal at Pipers Pool; the auction of produce --by a professional auctioneer – at Central, when Bob spent a fortune, in the process of trying to push the bidding up! All the meals that we had been given as we preached around the Circuit, and above all else, the wonderful welcome we were given by everyone – church folk and the townspeople as well.

At the end of June 1991, Paul and Therese had said their farewells to us, and had left for Omaha, Nebraska, U.S.A., where Paul was to do some research as part of his contract with hospitals in the Lancaster area; so for a whole year, there was a telephone hot line between Launceston and Omaha. That Christmas was the first one since their marriage when we had not met up at some stage of the holiday season; however, we did see David and Olga, John and Frances and their families, which was lovely. It was also a delight to welcome Rachael's friend, Samuel to our home. Samuel came from Newtownards, near Belfast, Northern Ireland, and they had met when they were students at Cliff College; we had a lovely New Year with him in our home.

All too soon, it was time for Rachael to go back to Lancaster; this time, Bob and I planned to stay in a motorway hotel overnight before returning home; this was one of the few occasions that Bob and I spent on our own, but it was marred by Bob's weariness after the long journey.

As the spring went on, it became more and more obvious that Rachael was very unhappy at Lancaster, this was due mainly to the music course she was doing – it was not what she expected and as a result, she had not settled at all. Bob felt she should stick it out, but in the end resigned himself to the fact that she would leave before the end of her first year.

Easter 1992 was a joyous occasion; Rachael and Samuel got engaged, much to everyone's delight, and on the same day, Samuel heard that he had been accepted for training for the Methodist Ministry, and would start at Wesley House, Cambridge, that autumn.

Sarah and Grandma had a break with different friends in Cheltenham and Bob and I went to Cliff College for the annual Dunamis Renewal Fellowship Weekend. We had a wonderful time, and came back feeling refreshed and renewed in every way. At this meeting we met up with a group from Jennymount Methodist Church, Belfast, and within days of arriving home, Bob was asked to preach there in August.

All this time, Bob was keeping reasonably well; and enjoyed many visits from friends; it was a real delight to welcome Carolyn Scholl from Maryland, U.S.A. for a long weekend, before she met up with friends to tour England, and not long after, to welcome Paul and Therese back from Omaha, into our new home for the first time. We were also pleased to see Ivan Wilson, Bob's friend from Cliff and his wife, Zandra, home on holiday from Canada.

Our trip to Belfast was wonderful and we had a very happy stay with Rev David Kilpatrick and his wife, Chris and four young sons. We arrived on the Friday, and were given the loan of a car for the weekend. The Saturday saw us driving up the Antrim coast to the Giant's Causeway; we had a lovely day, spoiled only by the heavy rain. The Sunday services were excellent, and on the Monday, David took us for a beautiful drive, taking in Newry, the Mountains of Mourne, Warren Point, Newcastle, and back to Belfast. Barbara Breen had taken us out on the Sunday afternoon to visit the place where St Patrick had (according to legend) kept his sheep (or pigs!), we had returned via Carrickfergus and saw the impressive castle on the water's edge; so all in all, we saw an awful lot in a short space of time; if you add to that, the reunion with the Dunamis group on the Friday night, and the meal with Samuel's family in Newtownards on the Monday night, then you can imagine what a memorable weekend we had; we left on the Tuesday morning, vowing to return as soon as possible.

The following weekend was August Bank Holiday, and all the family came together. Little did we realise that this would be the last one in which Bob could participate.

The new Methodist year of 1992/1993 started well; not least because our main church, Central, had decided to have the Church itself totally refurbished. The decision was made because the floor had to be completely replaced, and it was felt the right time to change the seating etc. The final service would be at the end of October, and worship would continue in the Church Hall until the job was done.

The weekend of 18th October saw Bob in great pain, he had not been quite as well since our trip to Belfast, but we had not paid too much attention to it, on the Friday his back was hurting so badly, that he had to lay down; the Saturday saw no improvement, and a visit to the doctor did little to help. Someone offered to take his Sunday morning service at Kennards House, but the evening service at Central was Holy Communion, and he insisted on doing it. He could barely walk and had to use a stick, but took most of the service sitting down - I helped as far as I possibly could. Monday saw another visit to the doctor and again on Tuesday; eventually, he was sent on Tuesday afternoon to Freedom Fields Hospital, Plymouth, where he remained for over two weeks. The diagnosis was a compression of the spinal cord due to the cancer in the spine; and the decision was made that he retire from the active Ministry immediately.

Bob had been home barely two weeks, when he was once more taken into hospital in Plymouth; this time Derriford, and by ambulance – sirens blaring. He had felt unwell in Church. I took him home and sent for the doctor; the pulmonary embolism was quite serious and could have caused his death, but thankfully, it was brought under control and Bob came home after a week.

From that point on, Bob worked hard at his walking; having come home needing to use a wheelchair, he progressed to a walking frame, and by Christmas was using one stick.

On the 1st December, we were visited by David Watson, from the Methodist Ministers' Housing Society; recognising our need of a more suitable house, they were prepared to sort out our retirement home straight away. Bob and I were told to look for a suitable place, within a defined price range, and four days before Christmas, we found a home that was situated on the other side of Launceston to the Manse, and only about half a mile from the town centre.

Being built on a slope, it appeared to be a bungalow from the front but in fact had some rooms downstairs. Upstairs was a two-bedroomed bungalow, but the four rooms downstairs were versatile; eventually they became another bathroom, a study, another sitting room, and a bedroom.

All the legal issues were dealt with by the London office, and we were eventually given the moving date of 15th March; this gave us a few days to decorate, and the whole circuit got involved; someone told Bob "It's just like Anneka Rice, here!" This referred to the television programme where Anneka was challenged to get a job done in a very short space of time.

Chapter Twenty Nine

In the last few days before we moved, Bob began to deteriorate; he had been in hospital in February to sort out pain control and then went to the Hospice at St Austell for four days, but was only home for a week when, the day before we were due to move, it became obvious that he had had another compression of the spinal cord. He was taken into the small hospital in Launceston, on the Sunday morning, and remained there for six weeks.

Bob loved our retirement home, but neither of us like its name – St Vincent. Independently of each other, we came up with 'Asbury' and decided that it was exactly what we wanted; it was a link with our American friends and with Methodism in general. Whenever anyone asked: "Why Asbury?" Bob would delight in giving the enquirer a brief lecture in Methodist history, reminding them that Francis Asbury was sent by John Wesley to work in America; that he worked tirelessly for forty-five years, and that, in the United States, he is almost more revered than Wesley himself.

Bob came home from hospital at the end of April, and the next day a group representing each of the churches in our section, and all the Circuit Stewards, met in the house to give Bob an official farewell from the Circuit; we received a handsome cheque, which helped a great deal in the work that had to be done in the house.

Life began to settle into a routine. In the morning, Bob was bed bathed, initially by me, but later on, by District Nurses. Once up and dressed, he would sit in his wheelchair, writing letters, or reading until after lunch, when he went back on the bed for a couple of hours, getting up again in the late afternoon, until about 8.30 p.m. – 9 p.m., when the long process of putting him to bed, began. It was usually about midnight when I got to bed.

The fact that Bob was totally paralysed from the waist down, meant that he was doubly incontinent; initially, this was a great problem to Bob, and he wept on many occasions, because he hated my having to deal with it; but we soon realised that this comparatively minor problem was going to take over our lives, if we didn't deal with it. Bob agreed that he would do the same for me if our roles were reversed, and eventually accepted that

I wanted to keep him at home, as much as he wanted to be there, and this was just a minute part of that plan.

From the moment Bob had been taken ill in the October, a never-ending stream of hot meals arrived, day by day on our doorstep, and people still brought in 'food parcels', which delighted Bob – he couldn't believe how much people loved him. Their love was also shown in the rota of lifts arranged to get me to the hospital in Plymouth; my driving was lacking experience to say the least, and it was a great weight off my mind to be taken to see Bob each day.

Throughout his illness, Bob never complained; he was always appreciative of all that was done for him, and never failed to say so. Many people felt that he didn't want to be bothered with the day to day running of the Circuit, but he would have loved to have been involved and to have known what was going on; he never mentioned this to anyone and only told me just weeks before he died.

During the whole of Bob's final illness, we were also preparing for Rachael and Samuel's wedding on 6th August. It took us all our time to get ourselves organised in the house; moving for a second time into a smaller home than the one before is not an easy task, and we had never quite come to terms with all our possessions in the Manse; it was even more difficult in our new home! Samuel spent the last six weeks before the wedding with us – he worked really hard, and it paid off; by 6th August we were more or less organised.

Bob had been doing very well; in fact there were times when he really seemed to be improving. He managed to get to church most Sundays, although it meant an early start, as we had to start to leave the house at 9.45 a.m. in order to have the time to get him in and out of the car and settled in the church ready for the 10.30 a.m. service. He was delighted to have been present both at the first service in the newly refurbished Church, and at the official opening services, but even more thrilled, when Chris Paxman, a Local Preacher from Central, asked if he would like to preach at the evening service he was due to take on 13th June. The service went well, and Bob's only disappointment was that he could not wear a clerical collar or his suit – the steroids he was taking had made him gain too much weight.

Before he was taken ill, Bob had been asked to be the Chairman for the annual Wesley Day Service at Altarnun, a short distance from

Launceston. From the moment he was taken ill, he had told Rev Keith Roberts, the superintendent Minister of the North Hill Circuit, of which Altarnun is a part, that he wasn't fit enough to do it. Keith, a good friend, whose support was greatly valued during Bob's illness, refused to take Bob's name off the programme, saying "We want you; if you can't make it, we'll have Joy; if she can't make it, I'll do it myself." Bob made it; and led the service from his wheelchair, and that service is remembered to this day.

Three weeks before he died, Bob spoke at a fellowship group, at the home of Mary and Ernie Rich, two other people whose support was invaluable. As we journeyed to see them, Bob, as usual, was telling me how to drive! When I told him that I drove much better when I was on my own, he said that he didn't know what I was talking about, and that "you've all the making of being an excellent driver - if you just do as I tell you!"

At the meeting, he talked quite frankly of his health, his faith, and the fact that now his funeral service was planned, he could get on with his life, living one day at a time. He was in great pain that evening, but determined to go, and in the end, it turned out to be the last time he spoke in public. Many people were blessed by his witness that night.

Rachael came home from Cambridge whenever she could; she was training as a Pharmacy Technician at Addenbrookes Hospital, a job she applied for when it was known that Samuel was to be a Student Minister at Wesley House, also in Cambridge. She came home for the last weekend before she stopped work for the wedding, and left Bob, as chirpy as ever, although he was very tired – he had spent four days in respite care at Launceston Hospital, and found the system for moving him from his bed to the wheelchair etc. exhausting – he was too used to the primitive system we used at home! When she returned on the Friday evening, Bob was far from well.

June and Dennis Carter, very old friends of Bob's, who first met him when he was a Student Minister, called on us unexpectedly that afternoon, and Bob had trouble communicating; they realised immediately that he was very ill indeed – I was still clutching at straws and hoping that whatever the problem was, it would wear off, and he would soon return to the form of normality that we had become used to over the last few months. Although he didn't appear to deteriorate over the next 24 hours, he certainly didn't improve, and the local G.P. warned us that this could be the beginning of the end, I refused to believe it until I heard it from our own G.P's lips. I did, however, blurt out to Rachael and Samuel that Sunday morning, (the wedding was due to take place on the Friday of that week) that he might not even be alive then let alone be at the wedding.

Our G.P. came back from his holiday, and immediately came to see Bob on the Tuesday. He talked to me for a long time before he saw Bob, and told me that it was either secondaries on the brain or a total metabolic breakdown due to the number of drugs Bob had been taking; either way, he just had a few days. He warned me not to take Bob to the wedding, because he couldn't guarantee that he wouldn't die during the service; however, he would do all he could to keep him going for as long as possible.

First thing Wednesday morning, I plucked up courage to suggest to Bob that he should stay at home while the wedding took place; considering that even first thing that morning, he was still talking about going, he took it very well, and readily agreed to stay at home, preserve his strength and be ready to meet everyone who came back to the house at 5 p.m. He began to write a greeting to be read out at the wedding, but he deteriorated rapidly that day.

All through that week, we alternated between laughing at the confused things Bob was saying, and crying at the heart wrenching events that were going on, especially when he was lucid.

We warned his mother that he was very ill, but it broke her heart when she saw him. She arrived here during the Thursday evening, and planned to stay for two weeks.

The morning of the wedding dawned, and we all went through the motions of getting ready. All week we had been doing what had to be done, but there was no sense of excitement as with a normal wedding. All the planned 'dummy runs' had fallen by the wayside, and we just got ourselves ready as best we could. I had not had much sleep that night; Bob had talked incessantly; every time I asked him to stop he just paused for a couple of minutes, and carried on. Eventually I yelled at him to shut-up – he said, "Sorry, darling" and carried on!! I do believe, however, that it was during that night, that the final battle was won, and he accepted his death. I well remember his chastising himself over and over again that he had wasted so many opportunities to witness for his

Lord; and then words I will never forget: "Look at the eyes of Jesus, and He did nothing (wrong)". It was as if he was meeting his Lord and seeing how sinless Jesus is, but how unworthy Bob himself felt.

Our good friends, Bob and Jenny Richards, Peter and Julie arrived in plenty of time for the wedding; Bob was the official photographer and made sure that he took some photos of Rachael, Sarah, me and Bob. Just as the bridesmaids were ready to leave, Bob called me; he had been trying to give me something all morning, but I had been rushing around, and kept telling him I'd see to it later. When I went over and took it, I saw that it was a clean handkerchief. "At least take <u>something</u> of me with you", he said; I left the room, told Rachael and Sarah and we all stood and cried.

Rev Kathleen Bowe, a tutor from Cliff College, took the service and a few minutes before the bride arrived, announced at our request, that Bob just had days to live, and was too ill to attend. Many people were shocked at the news because two weeks before, Bob had been doing so well.

Rachael had asked me to give her away in place of her Dad, and after our tears at home, we were fine. I really wanted her to have a special day, even though it could not be isolated from all that was going on at home.

The wedding service was lovely; we taped it, and played it to Bob that evening, although most of it went over his head. The Reception was held in the Church Hall, and the food organised by the ladies from the Church; it was lovely. The whole afternoon went well although there was no real hilarity; the speeches were good, but serious, and all were brief; in fact just right for the occasion.

Many people came back to the house, including a great number from Cheltenham, who had been at the service, and wandered around until the Reception was over and then came to spend the evening with us. Bob greeted everyone by name, although he was incapable of much more conversation than that. When we knew he was dying, I had said to Rachael: "Well, I've always believed that God's timing is perfect, but I think he's got it wrong this time." She replied: "No he hasn't, this way, Dad will see everyone who means anything to him, for one last time." I have to admit, she was right; everyone did see Bob that day, and he did enjoy himself in a limited way. A friend commented that Bob must have felt very loved that day.

Keith and Judith Roberts, our friends from the North Hill Circuit, sat with Bob while the wedding was going on, and we were very grateful – Bob was well looked after, and entertaining, too. Judith wrote it all down for us when she got home.

The Saturday saw a lot of final farewells. John went back to his work in Germany; friends popped in to say goodbye, and Rachael and Samuel set off for the honeymoon in the Lake District. That evening, Bob was trying to ask me for something, it was bedtime, and we were both tired, but I couldn't work out what he wanted; in the end, with tears streaming down my cheeks, I had to say: "I'm sorry, Darling, I can't understand what you're saying, but we'll work our way through until I do." I can still remember the look he gave me; for a few seconds he was totally lucid, and the love and compassion in his eyes will be with me always. It was the last moment that we were together in the true sense of the word, and deep down, I knew it; I left the room, and cried on Therese's shoulder.

Throughout the Sunday, Bob's health deteriorated. Paul and Therese had brought Aidan Robert, their first child, and Bob's first grandson (who was just six weeks old) to see Bob for the first time, but, thrilled as he was at his birth, he couldn't take it in when he finally saw him. Now they were staying for Bob's last days with us. We were warned that Bob would not last the night, and we decided to stay up. Bob's mother and a family friend, Viola, were staying with friends from the church, but that night, they decided to stay with us.

The G.P. on duty came and spoke to Paul, giving him medication to administer to Bob through the night. We played his favourite tape of worship songs (including "There is a Redeemer" which meant so much to him), throughout the night; and although he showed no signs of hearing us, we talked to him and prayed with him.

The District Nurse arrived in the morning, and spent a long time making him comfortable; I eventually went in, to sit with him, some time after 10.30 a.m. By now, feeling very weary, I sat beside the bed, holding his hand, my head on the bed, and I dozed off. It was good to be alone with him. Joy, Bob's sister Mary's daughter, was on holiday (arranged around the wedding) and arrived to see us at 11.10 a.m; she came in with a cup of coffee for me, and Paul joined her. Both working in the medical profession, they saw the signs before I realised what was happening, they pushed me closer and I whispered in Bob's ear: "I love you so much my Darling, but now it's time to say goodbye. I don't want you to go, but it's right that you do. I'll always love you Bob, as long as I live. Goodbye Darling". Within seconds, Bob was gone. It was 11.26 a.m. 9th August, 1997.

Many people have written, saying why Bob was so special to them, as a friend and as a Minister, but it's right to close with words that are Bob's taken from a Covenant Service address at St Mark's, Cheltenham.

I believe the Methodist Year, in Britain, is just right. It corresponds to the Academic Year in our state school system. It means that for those Methodist Ministers who have moved Circuits, today is their first appointment, their first service in their 'new' churches.

At St Mark's we celebrate this Annual Covenant Service today, as we shall do this evening in a United Covenant Service for Shipton and Andoversford, at Shipton. Whilst many churches still observe Covenant Sunday on the first Sunday in January, we feel that weather-wise, and for relevance, today is as good a day as any; and, in fact, it is close to the date of 11th August, 1755, on which the first, formal, Methodist Covenant Service was held, in the French Church at Spitalfields. The start of a New Methodist Year!

Whilst for the rest of us, neither starting school, nor changing schools nor facing "new" job prospects, again Covenant Sunday has something to say to you.

At the very end of the Covenant Liturgy, you will be invited to share in the Covenant Renewal – Fresh promises on our part, to serve God and our fellow men.

There are those Methodists who criticise the Covenant service – they did when John Wesley first introduced it; and there are some Methodists today, who never celebrate the Covenant. There are reasons for this; the main one is that there are those who hold that Covenant Services are too intensely personal in tone, to be used publicly. People who hold this view, might concede that the words of the Covenant service have their place in private devotion, but they are inappropriate as acts of corporate worship.

There is another criticism put forward. Some say that Covenant Services are unnecessary because a once-for-all Covenant has been made in Baptism. Whilst we hold that the promises made in

Baptism are vitally important, and that in a real sense, we enter into a Covenant relationship with God, in this Covenant Service today, we are not creating new Covenants, we are simply renewing the Covenant, which indeed is entered into at Baptism. The main emphasis today, must therefore be on renewal – fresh promises and pledges on our part.

Going back to the argument put forward, that the Covenant Service is too intensely personal, the high point of that comes almost at the very end, and that's why I put as a title for this short address, the opening words of the Covenant which we are invited to make.

"I AM NO LONGER MY OWN, BUT YOURS"

That's the most challenging thing expected of each one of us today, and these haunting words plumb the depths of our being. "I am no longer my own, but yours." How many of us, hand on heart, can honestly and truly say that that is true for me. For me? For me? I can't answer for you.

It might well be true that the word 'COMMITMENT' is overlooked, but the idea which it expresses is vitally important in the Christian life. Some weeks ago, I gave a definition of what it means to be a Christian which you won't find in any of the Historic Creeds of the Church or Catechisms. Here it is again:

"A Christian is a person who has ceased to do what he wants to do, and has begun to do what Jesus wants him to do." "I am no longer my own, but yours."

Being a Christian is not a hobby or a pastime – it is a total lifestyle. Jesus does not ask us for a part of our lives; nor even for large sections of them: He invites us to follow Him without reserve, to commit ourselves to Him completely.

"I am no longer my own, but yours."

David Watson, a leading figure in the Charismatic Movement, was an Anglican priest. He died of cancer, last year, aged about 50. In 1981 he wrote a book, which he called simply 'DISCIPLESHIP', and in one part he compared the attitude and approach of an

Olympic athlete with someone going as a spectator to the Olympics.

If someone is chosen to represent his country for the Olympics, his whole attitude and approach to his event will be quite different from someone who has himself chosen to go as a spectator.

With the athlete, there will be a total and sacrificial dedication to the task, partly because of the privilege of having been chosen. There will be a strong sense of responsibility which even the most enthusiastic tourist or ardent spectator will not have.

"I am no longer my own, but yours. Do with me whatever you will, let me simply trust and obey you in everything."

Jesus said in the Gospel, to those people who were considering becoming His disciples, and His words come right across the centuries and are addressed, spoken, to every one of us:

"If anyone would come after me, let him deny himself, and take up his cross and follow me."

Our response to that – "I am no longer my own, but yours."

Frances Schaeffer said:
"This is not an age in which to be a soft Christian."

True! But it is a tremendous joy and privilege to have been called to follow Jesus – and today, we renew our Covenant.

"I am no longer my own, but yours." AMEN.

Acknowledgements

My grateful thanks to Alison White, Rosemary Fawthrop,
Margaret Allwood and Mary Street
for their support and guidance in the preparation of this book.